# Surrogacy or Conspiracy?

## The Lamitina Story

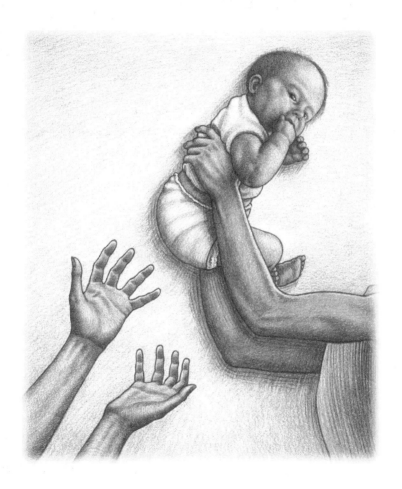

*By Gwyn & Tom Lamitina*

# Surrogacy or Conspiracy?
## The Lamitina Story

Contact:
Gwyn and Tom Lamitina
407-366-3349
tomlambo2004@aol.com

ISBN 978-0-615-27332-7 (alk. paper)

Book Design by Whitney Campbell, wcdesign@maine.rr.com
Cover Illustration by Rick Powell, rick@studiopowell.com
Editing by Eric Broder, erictbroder@yahoo.com

# Table of Contents

# Chapter 1

# The Start of a Surrogacy Journey

2

This is the story of our second surrogacy journey. Our first surrogacy resulted in a beautiful son, and we thought that since we had done this before, it would be a great success like the first time. Going back to the same surrogacy website where we found our first surrogate sounded simple enough. But even though we had done all this before, we soon discovered we didn't know as much as we thought we did.

We didn't know that predators are just waiting to take advantage of desperate people like us, intended parents that would do anything to have a child, and I mean anything. We thought we were smart. We took all the precautions available to protect ourselves as best we could. We did our homework on the person we chose to carry our child. But we soon found that sometimes even that is not enough.

It was even more disturbing to learn that even if we had a lawyer draw up the contract for this surrogacy, the laws in the state of Florida,where we lived, would not protect us from the tragedy that happened to us. We were doing a traditional surrogacy (using the surrogate's egg). The state of Florida is friendly only to gestational surrogacy (where the surrogate is implanted with an embryo). Laws relating to surrogacy vary from state to state. In Florida, the law on surrogacy is based on gestational surrogacy; the laws relating to traditional surrogacy revert to adoption laws.

We felt like a gestational surrogacy was pretty much a gimme, anyway. If the egg used is not the egg of the surrogate, but is the intended mother's egg or a donated egg, then the surrogate has no biological right to the baby. But when doing a traditional surrogacy, it gets a little unclear regarding who has what rights when things go wrong – unless you specifically antic-ipate every little thing that could possibly go wrong. This is, as you will see, a story with many twists and turns. And even though we are writing about this story, the story is not over.

Our little girl had just turned one year old when we saw her for the first time. We hadn't seen her in person; instead we saw what she looks like for the first time on the television show *Inside Edition*. What a cutie. It has been so hard not being able to see her grow, missing all of her firsts – first smile, first words, first steps. We've missed all of those milestones, and have not been able to be involved in any part of her life. For that matter, we can't even share with her how much we love her, or that we even exist.

Before we go further on this journey, we want to share our story in the hope of preventing this from happening to anyone else. If we can save just one couple from going through what we did, this book will have been worth writing.

## Why Surrogacy?

Before Tom and I were married, I had been married and had a son. Doctors were not quite sure how this happened since I had irregular menstrual cycles and endometriosis.

This caused me a lot of pain and left me anemic; the menstrual cycles would go for 10 days, and were heavy almost till the end. Women who have been through this know the pain can be so debilitating that you can miss days of work each month, along with dealing with all the other symptoms that go with it.

Something had to be done. I went back and forth with my doctor, trying different treatments, trying everything but the dreaded hysterectomy or partial hysterectomy. Finally, after suffering enough, I accepted my doctor's recommendation that we go ahead and do the hysterectomy. At that time, in the '80s, they really didn't have any other alternatives. Doctors still thought PMS was all in your head.

The doctor and I decided that he would perform a partial hysterectomy; at least by keeping my ovaries I would not have to take hormones for the rest of my life. Even doing a partial hysterectomy was no guarantee – more tumors might reappear, and they would have to go back and remove my ovaries as well.

So this gives a little bit of background into why I can't have more biological children. When I met Tom, he had never been married and had no children of his own. For me it would have been okay to adopt a child – I knew I would be doing that anyway, no matter which way we went. But it was important to Tom to have a child that was biologically related to one of us.

## Our First Success

We had been looking for a year and a half on the Internet, trying to find a surrogate, when we happened upon the surrogacy website **www.surro-momsonline.com**. Women all over the country place ads on this website, advertising to be surrogate moms for couples who can't conceive on their own. There we found our first surrogate. She had placed an ad on the website and we answered it.

We talked over the Internet for a while, then several times on the phone. We decided that we should meet. We hit it off right from the start and the rest was history, as they say. We had a beautiful baby boy that came from this wonderful relationship between our surrogate and us.

To us, the surrogate of our son was an angel sent by God. We plan to be open and honest with our son, and explain to him when he gets older so that he understands what a sacrifice this woman made to have a child for us, a child she so lovingly gave to us to raise as our own. To tell this surrogate, our friend, thank you, just is not enough to convey how much her generosity meant to us. This was a person who, until we started this surrogacy journey, had been a stranger, and has now become a member of our family forever.

You can't share something like this and not become close. It takes a very special person to be a surrogate. Not everyone can or should be one. It takes a selflessness and amazing strength to give up a child, especially when that child is biologically related to you, as the surrogate. We can only imagine the turmoil and emotions that you go through. Even as we write this, it is so hard to express how we feel as intended parents that you give so much and take so little. So thank you to all of you who help provide a family for those who otherwise could not have children on their own.

## The Quest For Another Child

We always knew that after our first son was born we wanted to have another child. Our son was such a blessing to us, how could we not want another child? Our son lights up our lives every day, and he is so alive. He is one of the best things that ever happened to us.

So when our son was almost two years old, we decided to approach our previous surrogate to do another surrogacy for us. We had such a wonderful experience with her. But she was undecided on whether or not she would want to be a surrogate again. She had four children of her own and had complications with our son while carrying him. She developed a full placenta previa: The placenta was blocking the way for the baby to be born vaginally. Luckily we found out early in her pregnancy, but because of this our son was delivered almost two months early and our surrogate could have died due to complications. Doctors had to do an emergency C-section.

Our previous surrogate was not sure that she wanted to do another surrogacy and she was thinking of retiring. Who could blame her? She was raising her four children on her own and she decided she didn't want to risk the chance of possibly having another child and again experiencing placenta previa, which is likely to recur. It was hard for all of us to come to this decision because she is and always will be like family.

So, we decided to go back to the same website where we found our first surrogate to look for a second surrogate. We began contacting the persons in the ads by e-mail, going through the same process as we had done so many times before. For whatever reasons, not everybody you talk to wants to do a surrogacy with you, or you with them. Contrary to what critics have thought about us, we did do background investigations on both the first and second surrogates who we chose to carry our children. We were unable to find anything worrisome in the background of either surrogate — at least not by the means available to us. Obviously, the key is finding a surrogate who you can trust. It all boils down to trust.

My husband saw an ad that caught his eye on this website. The woman lived right here in Florida, had a reasonable fee of $15,000, and said in her ad that she was experienced.

The original ad that the surrogate placed on the website was documented in court records and reads as follows:

TS looking for IP's. I am a 28 year old experienced surrogate (one TS-'02 and one GS-'04) and egg donor (three times) in addition to having and raising my own two children. I also have my bachelor's degree in elementary education. I am looking to be a first year teacher this coming school year. I am not looking for much in the way of compensation, but am looking for the "right" couple that has the following: MUST BE HETEROSEXUAL. Be willing to pay for medical insurance or wait until Sept/Oct. Be willing to pay for maternity clothing. I have some maternity clothes, but the majority of them are not suitable for teaching. Be willing to pay for lost wages due to postpartum or bed rest. Be willing to have some inseminations done (free) in my home town. Be willing to seriously consider home birth (I will take off the cost of this from my compensation). Be willing to have an open relationship before/during/after. Be honest. Only wants a TS (cannot do a GS due to a reaction to medication). Be willing to pay a reasonable compensation. BE SERIOUS. Please send only serious replies that match most or all of the above to my e-mail address.

# Chapter 2

# How the
# Surrogacy Began

We began to think: could this be the one? We contacted this woman by e-mail just as we had done countless others, and started an ongoing conversation with her. This woman – we'll call her Jennifer; not her real name – was a little younger than our previous surrogate had been and so we thought she could possibly be our surrogate for more than one child. We had several more conversations with Jennifer through e-mail and then by telephone. We decided to meet in person.

We were so excited at the possibility of another surrogacy and having a sibling for our son. We all decided to get together at Jennifer's home and discuss in more detail our expectations of her, and hers of us, to see if this was a commitment we both wanted to make. We hoped Jennifer would become a part of our family, just as our first surrogate had and still is today.

So Jennifer e-mailed us her address and Tom and I began to daydream about doing this surrogacy, going on doctor's visits with Jennifer, looking at our baby on the 3-D ultrasound machine and watching it grow. We had done a 3-D ultrasound of our son when our previous surrogate was pregnant and it was literally like taking the baby out of the womb, taking pictures of him, and then putting him back in the womb – it was amazing!

We set up a date to go to Jennifer's home in Jacksonville, Florida. When we arrived, Jennifer invited us in and we sat down to get down to the specifics of what we expected from each other. We had mentioned to Jennifer in previous e-mails that we had done a surrogacy before, and that we were not married but were planning to get married later in the year. We let her know that we had been living together for more than 17 years. We were not just a couple who had only been together a few years and then decided to have a child; we had been together for a long time. We wanted Jennifer to feel comfortable with her decision to pick us as intended parents.

During the discussion with Jennifer, I mentioned that we had frozen eggs left over from our previous surrogacy and I wanted to know if she would consider doing a gestational surrogacy. She then said that she was allergic to the medications required to do a gestational surrogacy.

Jennifer reminded me that she had stated this in the ad she had placed on the web site. I apologized that I wasn't aware of this, as Tom had found the ad and contacted Jennifer, and I hadn't actually read the ad. While we were discussing the contract and what each of us wanted in the contract, Jennifer began to tell us some things about herself and her family. She was a divorced single mom and had two children, a girl and a boy.

But there was a third child living there in her home. When we asked her about this child, Jennifer told us this child was the result of the gestational surrogacy she mentioned in her ad. She had done this gestational surrogacy for her roommate Sue (not her real name), as Sue had not been able to get pregnant. She also told us that Sue was also Jennifer's alleged adoptive mother.

At the time of this visit, we got to meet Jennifer's daughter and Sue's son, but we didn't get to meet Jennifer's older son. She explained that he was playing video games in another room and when he was playing those games you could forget about him coming out for a while. So in that first meeting, we never did meet her older son.

Tom and I discussed with Jennifer what we were expecting from her as a surrogate. We explained that we wanted a surrogate that did not smoke, drink, or take drugs, and that it was important that there be no history of a genetic disorder in her family that could be passed on to the baby. Above all, we wanted there to be trust between us. Without trust, an arrangement like this is not going to work.

Jennifer assured us that none of our expectations were a problem. She reminded us that she had mentioned the need for honesty in her surrogate ad. Jennifer asked us if we had planned for her to stick to a strict diet before and during the pregnancy. We told her that we would like her to eat healthy, of course, but that we would not ask her to stick to a specific diet.

We offered to give her the phone number of our first surrogate so she could call and talk to her about her surrogacy with us, but she replied that it would not be necessary. We also offered Jennifer copies of medical records of Tom's test for any sexually transmitted diseases and our psychological profile that she could review and give to her midwife and OB/GYN; she said she would get back to us on whether or not she would need that information.

We agreed that we both wanted to proceed with the surrogacy, and Jennifer suggested we get started right away. She asked us which one of us wanted to draw up the contract for the surrogacy. We suggested that she do it because she had access to Microsoft Word and at the time we did not. We also suggested to Jennifer that there were contract templates on the website where she had posted her ad that it would give her the basics. All she would have to do is enter the information as it pertained to our situation.

We told Jennifer that our former surrogate had used that method to produce our first contract. Jennifer agreed and said that she would take care of it. Jennifer suggested we start right away with the in-home inseminations. We'd need to start in two weeks as this would be the time she would be producing an egg to be fertilized. So we set up a date and time to come back to Jennifer's home to give her a first sample for insemination. On the way home my husband and I were thinking that this surrogacy might even be better than the first, if that was possible.

We lived in Georgia when we did the first surrogacy and our first surrogate lived in Tampa, Florida, so it was difficult for us to be able to get to all the doctor's visits. But this time was going to be different. We lived closer to this second surrogate and we hoped things would go better during this pregnancy, she wouldn't develop complications, and we would get to see the baby born.

As I mentioned earlier, the first surrogate gave birth to our son two months early after being rushed to the hospital for an emergency C-section, so by the time we got to the hospital she had already had our son. This time, we had high hopes that we would be able to be even more involved in the pregnancy.

Finally, after a long two weeks, it was time for us to drop off the first sample to Jennifer. As we prepared to do this, we talked about how it would be neat to have a girl this time. But Tom and I both agreed we didn't care as long as the baby was healthy.

Jennifer had suggested that we get there right before her bedtime so she could stay in bed once the sample was inserted. Since it was a drive of more than two hours to her home in Jacksonville from our home in Orlando, I suggested to my husband that I would stay home to make sure our son got to bed on time.

While Tom was there for the first insemination, Jennifer suggested that there was a short window of time – just a few days – that she would be fertile, and that Tom should come back at least once and maybe twice more to take advantage of these few days that she was fertile. When doing home inseminations, it's hard to determine the most fertile days, even when menstrual cycles are regular.

So we agreed to make another trip two to three days later. My husband asked Jennifer at the time of this first insemination if she had the contract ready. She told him she was still working on it and that she would e-mail over the rough draft when it was completed for us to examine to make sure everything was as we liked it.

At this point we weren't too concerned that Jennifer hadn't finished the contract. We figured everyone was busy and since Jennifer and her room-mate/adoptive mother Sue were running a daycare out of their home, that took a lot of their time. So Tom went back to Jennifer's home two to three days later as planned, to bring another sample and take advantage of this first menstrual cycle as much as possible. It was at this time that Jennifer mentioned that we should plan to send my husband back the following month to do the inseminations again, just in case she didn't get pregnant on the first try. Meanwhile, we anxiously waited for our surrogate to inform us if we were going to be parents or not.

When we received the first "not pregnant" call from Jennifer, we were a little sad that the first time had not worked. We knew by doing the inseminations this way we were only estimating the time when the surrogate was most fertile every month, and because of that it could be a long process. We had heard of intended parents still trying a year later, and still childless.

We told Jennifer that we knew we needed to give this process at least four to six months before discussing what other options we might need to take at that point. We tried to go on with our lives, anticipating the next month and hoping for good news.

Now and then Jennifer would call us and we would call her, just trying to keep in touch and getting to know each other just a little bit better. During these conversations Jennifer began to share more with us about herself, her family, and her life. We were thinking that this journey was turning out to be a lot like the first; we felt so blessed. Little did we know what was ahead of us.

When it was time for the second month's insemination, my husband had planned to go to Jennifer's home to drop off another sample. But Jennifer suggested that she and Sue come to our house this time to do the inseminations. Well, we certainly didn't mind her coming to our home, but that was a long trip. Since Jennifer was nice enough not to charge us the normal fee for doing inseminations, we thought it was only right that we continue coming to her house to drop off the samples.

Jennifer insisted that it would be better if she came to our home to do the second insemination, because that way she would be able to get two inseminations back-to-back as opposed to getting them several days apart. We agreed and decided that we would take Jennifer to dinner at a restaurant we liked. When Jennifer, Sue, and Sue's son arrived at our home, we set off to go to the restaurant and they followed us in their car.

After the meal we came home, and since Jennifer liked to be in bed by 8 p.m. every night, we showed the women where everybody would sleep. Jennifer decided she would sleep in the upstairs bedroom and Sue would sleep downstairs on the sleeper sofa.

While Jennifer and Sue were deciding where to sleep, Jennifer mentioned to us that the Sue's son had not been feeling well and they thought that he was coming down with a cold. Jennifer asked Sue if Sue's son would be sleeping with Sue, since he was not feeling well. Sue replied that her son would be sleeping with Jennifer, and that she was going to bed.

We thought that it was a bit odd that Sue – the biological mother of this child – would not want to take care of her one and only son when he was sick, but rather have Jennifer do it for her instead. After we got everyone situated where they wanted to sleep, Tom and I went to bed ourselves. As we talked about this oddity we just had witnessed, we discussed that it seemed that this child that was supposed to be Sue's child was really Jennifer's child.

If that was true, then Jennifer had never done a gestational surrogacy for Sue, as her ad had stated. This was just one of many bizarre things that occurred during our time with Jennifer and Sue. During that weekend, Jennifer asked us how much money we made. She commented that we must pull in a large paycheck to pay for our house, because it was three times the size of theirs. Jennifer also told us that she could afford a house like ours because her father had left her a million dollar inheritance, but she wanted to save it for the kids' college education fund.

More strange things started to emerge during this surrogacy. We caught some inconsistencies, but nothing that was proof positive that something was wrong. All we had was some odd behavior and an uneasy feeling. We made up our minds that if Jennifer didn't get pregnant after four attempts, we would find a way to bow out gracefully from this surrogacy. If she *did* get pregnant by then, we would get through the weird and bizarre behaviors and focus on what was best for the baby. We would forge on with the relationship, as long as these women's weird behavior didn't get any worse.

Jennifer called Tom while he was out of town on one of his business trips to let him know that he could come by her house to drop off an insemination on his way back home for our third try. Tom did just that, and we continued planning our wedding in Hawaii.

A month later, after the third insemination didn't take, we planned to do one more attempt with Jennifer. This would be our fourth and final insemination regardless of whether or not she got pregnant.

Tom went out of town on business before the fourth insemination was to take place. When we got a call from Jennifer asking Tom to come up to her house for the fourth try, Tom had been home from his trip for only one day and he mentioned to Jennifer that he had just returned home and was tired from the long trip. He wanted to know if he could skip this insemination. I suggested to Tom that he go ahead and give Jennifer this final insemination. If this fourth try didn't succeed, we would talk with her about the possibility of bowing out.

In the meantime we finally got approved for a home equity loan to pay for our wedding in Hawaii, our swimming pool, and the surrogacy. Once the loan was funded we set the date for our wedding in Hawaii.

Jennifer called Tom and asked if he had signed the surrogacy contract that she had sent us. He said no – we had temporarily misplaced the contract and were not able to find it at that present moment. We wondered what was the hurry. We had been trying to get Jennifer to change my last name on the contract to Hardman – my legal name at that time – since we first started four months earlier.

We had made Jennifer aware that she had put my husband's last name on the contract as my last name early on, and I would not be able to sign it or get it notarized until we were married and the name change was officially made. Jennifer said she would fax us the corrected page with the name changed to my former married name if we would just sign the contract before going out of town.

My husband reminded Jennifer that he was not home; he was out of town on business and she would have to call me so I could turn on the fax machine. When Jennifer called me, I asked her if this could wait until we returned from our trip because we were getting married and then she would not have to change the name on the contract because then I would legally have my husband's last name.

But Jennifer said no. She said her midwife had her signed copy and needed ours. The first time we did a surrogacy the doctor said the same thing. Under Florida law, the doctor had to have a signed contract before the surrogate could be seen. So I had Jennifer fax the signature page and when my husband returned home from business we both signed it, had it notarized, and then sent it back to Jennifer.

That is the reason we didn't get a signed copy of the contract with Jennifer's signature at that time. We knew from doing our first surrogacy that the physician or midwife for the surrogate needed a copy of the signed surrogacy contract to be able to give the surrogate medical care.

A copy of this fax and contract that was sent to us by Jennifer was documented in court records. At the top of the fax she sent us was her name, Sue's name, and their home phone number, dated 9/3/06.

So off to Hawaii we went to get married. After a long airplane ride we were finally in Hawaii. We checked into the resort and hurried to our room; we were tired from the flight but excited to be there.

As we were checking out the scenery from our balcony, there was a knock at the door. The concierge had a card and three balloons in his hand. It just so happened that Tom's birthday was that day, September 9th. Tom opened the card that came with the balloons and it said "Happy Birthday Tom! Congratulations on your wedding and new baby!" It was from Jennifer and Sue.

We were still half asleep because it was about 4 a.m. our time on the east coast, and when Tom looked at the card he didn't even finish reading the whole thing. He assumed it was for his birthday and the wedding. When Jennifer called us later to see if we received the card and balloons, Tom realized that the card had told us we were having a baby.

We were happy, but feeling a little apprehensive about how this pregnancy would go. The wedding was the next day. We were so happy to be having a dream wedding in Hawaii. We had been together for 17 years and it was about time to get married. The wedding was beautiful and we had two weeks to spend in Hawaii. It was wonderful – we couldn't have asked for more.

A two-year-old boy and a new baby on the way – life was good! When we got back home from our vacation, Tom had to go out of town on business. On his way, he dropped off a check for the first surrogate fee payment at Jennifer's house. Later he called and told me that Jennifer had called him while he was working, and wanted to come down to our house after he got back from his business trip

Jennifer told Tom that she had a teacher's workshop and conference to attend at the University of Central Florida on a Friday and wanted to stay at our home while attending the workshop. Since the university was so close, Jennifer said she would come over to our home on Thursday evening after work, spend the night, and attend the workshop on Friday morning.

Jennifer asked if Sue could bring the kids over on Friday night so they could take them to Sea World, which isn't far from our home, on Saturday morning. The Thursday after Tom returned from his business trip Jennifer was to come to our home. We arranged to have her meet us for dinner that night. When we got to the restaurant, Jennifer handed me a framed sonogram picture of our baby. It was too early to know the gender, but we were so excited to see that first picture.

At dinner, Jennifer told us about an incident that happened at her school that day. She said that one of her fifth grade students had brought a .38 caliber handgun, fully loaded, in his backpack and had planned to use it on some students and who knows who else.

We were shocked and understandably concerned at this point about the safety of the surrogate and the baby in this school. But Jennifer assured us that she thought this was an isolated incident. We weren't so sure, given the shootings involving students in schools across America these days.

That Friday morning Jennifer left early to attend her workshop. Tom and I had made plans to attend a conference of our own in another part of town.

Around 4 p.m. that day, Jennifer had returned to our home from her workshop. She called us to let us know she was waiting for us and wanted to know when we would be returning home. We explained that it might be a while, so we told her how to get into our home and disarm the alarm.

Thinking everything was okay at this point with Jennifer, we got ready to get back to the conference. Five minutes later, though, we got another call from her, telling us that she was hungry. Tom told her that she could microwave some food from the refrigerator or that there was food in the pantry – she could have whatever she wanted.

Jennifer said that she didn't want to do that; she didn't feel comfortable going through our refrigerator or our cabinets. We asked her if she could wait until we got home. She asked us how much longer were we going to be, and we told her that we would probably be a few more hours at the convention, then it would depend on the traffic as to how much longer from there.

Jennifer called us four more times from her cell phone and from our home phone. We could not figure out why this woman was calling us so much – not that we minded, but it seemed odd. Later it would become clear.

So we told Jennifer that if she was hungry she could order a pizza from a restaurant around the corner and have it delivered. When we got home we would reimburse her – that way Jennifer could eat, and Sue and the kids could eat when they got to the house. But Jennifer said she didn't have any money. So Tom told her to order the pizza and we would pick it up on our way home from the conference.

After this last phone call with Jennifer, Tom remarked to me that Jennifer said she didn't have any money to pay for the pizza, yet they were taking her children to Sea World the next day. It didn't make sense. So we decided that since the conference was coming to an end shortly, we would leave early to pick up the pizza and head home.

We brought the pizza home and by this time Sue had arrived with the children. I apologized that they had to wait for the pizza and invited them to come and dig in, as they must be starving. Jennifer then said to us that she wasn't that hungry. Tom and I looked at each other and rolled our eyes. Now she *wasn't* hungry?

Later, Tom and I talked about how many times this woman had called us while we were at the conference. Tom checked his cell phone to see how many times she had actually called us – it was a total of six.

Jennifer had been calling us every four or five minutes until the end when she waited about 45 minutes and then called again to see how far we were from the house and if we had picked up the pizza yet. So we wondered why she would call us this many times saying she was starving, and then, when we got home, say she wasn't hungry. We knew something was not quite right about this whole thing.

Early that next morning I was awakened by the sound of the front door opening – I heard the chiming sound that the alarm makes when you open and close the main doors of our house when the alarm isn't set.

Jennifer knew that we usually set the alarm at night before going to bed, but she had asked us not to that night, as they didn't want to wake us when they left in the morning. But on that Saturday morning, having been awakened by the chime, I looked out the window thinking that Jennifer, Sue, and the children must be getting an early start to Sea World.

But instead I saw Jennifer walking up the driveway with a lit cigarette in her hand. She proceeded to walk to the side of our house, presumably to finish the cigarette. I was stunned that she was smoking after she had told us she did not smoke. I worried about the health of the baby – didn't she care about the unborn child, too? After all, the baby was half hers biologically.

I looked over towards Tom lying in bed. The chimes hadn't woken him and I decided to let him sleep. When Tom did wake up, I told him that I had caught the surrogate smoking.

We discussed the concerns we had that Jennifer was smoking and possible repercussions to the baby. We wondered why Jennifer risked smoking at our house in the first place, unless she wanted to get caught. She could have driven somewhere or walked up the street to avoid the risk of us seeing her smoking.

It didn't make sense. But then nothing about this surrogate or this surrogacy made sense. The night before, Jennifer surprised us with the news that she carried a genetic birth defect that could possibly be passed down to our child. Her oldest son was affected by this genetic defect – the child she hadn't allowed us to see during that first meeting at her home. She had not divulged this worrisome fact in the beginning of this surrogacy.

Now we knew that Jennifer smoked and carried a genetic defect that could possibly affect our child. Our heads were spinning. She was almost two months pregnant. Why was she just now divulging this information to us, when she should have told us before we ever got started with this surrogacy? We had specifically asked Jennifer if she smoked and if there were any medical abnormalities in her family.

Jennifer, Sue, and the children got back late that night from Sea World. Jennifer told us they were tired and were going to bed.

I decided that I was going to go to bed myself since Tom was already there. Jennifer had not been back from Sea World for 10 minutes when I heard the alarm chime again. I looked through the curtains to check who was going outside.

Jennifer was sitting in her car, which was parked underneath the window of our bedroom. The inside light was on. I saw her grab a prescription pill bottle that contained what I assumed were her prenatal vitamins, then take one out and swallow it.

Then she grabbed a pack of cigarettes, took a cigarette out of the pack, grabbed a lighter to light the cigarette, and then proceeded to go to the side of the house to smoke the cigarette. I shouted, "Oh my God!" waking up Tom.

Tom asked me what was wrong and I told him that Jennifer was smoking again. Tom went out to see why Jennifer was smoking and when she saw him coming she took off back into the house, leaving the smoldering cigarette behind on the ground.

We were very upset and concerned about the safety of our child.

We were both so upset we felt we needed time to sleep on this, get up with a fresh perspective, and discuss it calmly in the morning. Little did we know that Jennifer, Sue, and the children would take off in the wee hours of the morning because they had no intention of talking to us.

I began to wonder if the events of this weekend had been planned out. This was the first weekend we had seen Jennifer since we found out that she was pregnant. She had waited until she was pregnant to divulge the potential birth defect and her smoking habit.

After they left, we began to look around the house for anything out of place. We discovered certain financial paperwork had been taken out of its place and not put back. Paperwork had been left lying on top of the other papers in the filing cabinet. Our thoughts immediately went back to the day before when Jennifer was alone in our house and calling us frequently to check where we were. Could she have been going through our financial papers at that time? If so, what was she looking for? Was Jennifer trying to find out how much we were worth and what Tom was making in salary every year?

Tom and I became very concerned that maybe this surrogacy was not what it should be. We both wanted to believe that maybe we were worried for nothing, and that Jennifer would call us and offer an explanation that would clear up our concerns. It never happened.

In fact, several days went by. We tried a couple of times to contact Jennifer on her cell phone and left a message on her home phone. She did not get back to us. I began to think that she had planned all of this from the beginning; she was pregnant, this child was part hers biologically – she had all the cards.

Why would Jennifer need to be worried about being caught smoking or revealing the genetic problems in her medical history, now that she was pregnant? What did she need to worry about? Nothing now, except maybe how much child support she was going to get from us.

Finally, after a week, Jennifer called us and told us what we had feared: she declared that this was her baby, and there was nothing we could do about it. We were pretty much going to have to do what she said to try and make it through this surrogacy.

Tom and I wanted to know why she would lie and say she didn't smoke when she did. He asked her just that: why she was smoking, especially while pregnant, when she had told us that she did not smoke? Jennifer said that she smoked one to two cigarettes a month whenever she had a migraine, that it was a remedy her midwife had given her permission to use to relieve the headaches. So Tom asked her how many cigarettes she had smoked that month. Jennifer replied that the cigarette she was smoking after the Sea World trip was the first one she had smoked this month.

Then Tom asked her why I had seen her smoking the morning before her trip to Sea World. In a very excitable tone she asked how could that be possible; it was 5 a.m. and we were sleeping. Tom replied that the chiming alarm of the front door opening had awakened me. He explained to Jennifer that we were very disappointed at her concealment of her smoking and the birth defect that ran in her family because, at least early on, we had hoped to use her for a third surrogacy in the future.

Jennifer replied by saying, "You do not want three children. I have three children, and they will all want to do different things, and then they're always arguing about everything. Trust me, you don't want three children." Tom said that this third child she had mentioned was not hers, it was Sue's – at least according to what she had told us.

Jennifer told him that she was taking care of this third child. So why, we thought, would Jennifer be taking care of a child that was not biologically hers? Could this be evidence? Was this a slip of the tongue that this third child was not the result of a gestational surrogacy using Sue's egg as she had claimed, but rather a traditional surrogacy Jennifer had done previously and kept … or could this be a love child?

We had a suspicion that this child was probably biologically related to Jennifer. It made sense now why Sue did not want to stay up with this third child when he was sick at our home the first time they came to visit. We had wondered why the child had been following Jennifer around and not Sue. It was starting to come together now.

As the conversation between Jennifer and Tom continued, she asked him what was the big deal about her smoking, anyway. She admitted that she smoked throughout her previous pregnancies and her own children turned out okay. Well, in our opinion that was still to be determined. Jennifer said that she used smoking as a way to relieve her migraines and that not smoking was far worse than the migraines themselves.

We thought smoking makes migraines worse. Nothing that this woman was telling us made sense. Jennifer asked us if it would have made a difference if she had told us in the beginning that she smoked. Of course we answered yes. We would have liked to have had a chance to make that decision ourselves first. Had we known in the beginning she smoked and had a genetic defect that could be passed down to our child, we would have not used her as a surrogate.

Tom and I came to the conclusion that Jennifer was going to smoke anyway and that we were not going to be able to stop her from doing that or anything else. In fact, Jennifer told us this wasn't going to work and we knew by this time we could not trust her.

We called the midwife to verify with her if what Jennifer was telling us was true. Jennifer told Tom that the midwife had given her permission to smoke cigarettes as a remedy for headaches. The midwife told us that she would not tell anyone to smoke while pregnant if she could help it, but she also said she was under medical confidentiality laws and unless Jennifer gave her written permission, she would not be able to discuss it with us. She went on to say that she had received verbal permission from Jennifer, but that wasn't enough – it had to be in writing.

We realized that we were going to be in a big mess for the remainder of this pregnancy. So we looked to the surrogacy contract to see what the remedies were for a breach of contract.

The contract stated specifically that when a breach occurred, a letter had to be sent by mail to the party that had breached the contract, stating what the breach was. We prepared this letter and sent it to Jennifer, following what we thought was proper procedure based on what was outlined in the contract, and then we sent a copy to her via e-mail as well.

We thought we were following the law and that the contract was a legal document recognized by the state of Florida since it was almost identical to the surrogacy contract we had used previously. Later we would find that it didn't do us much good. This is when the legal fight over the child began.

# Chapter 3

# The War of Words

$T$his is the Breach of Contract letter that was sent to Jennifer:

Breach of Traditional Surrogacy Contract

To: Jennifer,

This is an acknowledgement of a material breach of contract after confirmation of pregnancy as stated in Paragraph B of the Traditional Surrogacy Contract, on the part of the surrogate [surrogate's name] (hereinafter referred to as the "Surrogate") and the intended father Thomas James Lamitina (hereinafter referred to as the "Intended Father") and the intended mother Patricia Gwyn Hardman Lamitina (hereinafter referred to as the "Intended Mother"). The Intended Father and the Intended Mother are hereinafter collectively referred to as Intended Parents.

As the Traditional Surrogacy Contract paragraph H and sub-paragraph number 3 states, the surrogate agrees not to smoke any type of cigarettes, drink alcoholic beverages, or use illegal drugs, prescription or non prescription drugs, without the consent of the obstetrician or midwife. It has been confirmed by the midwife that she did not give the surrogate consent to smoke any cigarettes for migraines or any other condition as it could be unhealthy for the unborn child. Surrogate has confirmed that she does smoke cigarettes and has been since time of pregnancy.

This letter of breach of contract between surrogate and intended parents is in compliance with the Traditional Surrogacy Contract and is to inform the surrogate of such a breach in writing. The surrogate has stated that the breach cannot be cured that she will continue smoking for her alleged migraines.

It is the intention of the Intended Parents to take legal responsibility for the child and adoption at time of birth as long as said child is the biological child of the Intended Father and the child is checked out by a physician at time of birth and found to be healthy with no abnormalities due to smoking cigarettes. At that time if the child is healthy and the surrogate signs the rescission form to give up any legal ties to this child, the Intended Parents agree to pay the surrogate her surrogacy fee of $15,000 minus the $1500.00 first payment that was

31

already paid to the surrogate. The Intended Parents will also pay for maternity clothes at 12 weeks as agreed. Also, as it states in the original contract, the Intended Parents will send pictures once a year and the surrogate will be able to visit the child if she so chooses once or twice a year.

Sincerely,

Thomas James Lamitina
Patricia Gwyn Hardman Lamitina
(Intended Parents)

After a day or two Jennifer e-mailed the following response to the Breach of Contract letter:

Here is my response to your breech [sic] of contract:

**1)** It states that my midwife did not give me consent to smoke any cigarettes for migraines or any other condition. This statement is untrue. She did in fact give me permission to smoke cigarettes as alternative treatments to cure the migraines are considered more dangerous than that of smoking cigarettes.

Further, [the midwife] would not need to give me permission or consent as the FDA states that smoking less than 10 cigarettes per day should be considered "safe" at any stage of pregnancy, as per [the midwife].

**2)** I have decided to change doctors as no doctor needs to play "in between". I have further decided not to inform you of the new doctor of my choosing until after requested DNA testing confirms that you are the biological father of the child. Being that you are requesting the paternity testing, you have relinquished yourself from the priviledge [sic] of contacting my doctor during the pregnancy until after confirmation. At such time, someone will contact you to inform you of whom my new doctor is.

Due to the change in doctors, I will no longer qualify for a home birth since [the midwife] is the only certified midwife in Jacksonville and some surrounding counties. In the original contract, it states that if I give birth at home, I will receive a compensation fee of $15,000; if I deliver at a birthing center, I will receive a $18,000 compensation fee; if I deliver in a hospital, I will receive a $20,000 compensation fee. Therefore, due to the change in doctors, we are no longer looking at the $15,000 compensation fee.

**3)** It states in the Breech [sic] of contract that it is your intention to take legal responsibility at the time of birth if the child is checked out by a physician at the time of birth and found to be healthy with no abnormalities due to smoking cigarettes. You can have a doctor of your choosing to perform a physical on the baby, I also have the right to choose a doctor to perform the same or a similar test. Any findings must be backed by research documentation to prove that cigarettes alone caused any abnormalities.

**4)** It states in the Breech [sic] that the surrogate has stated that the breech [sic] cannot be cured that she will continue smoking for her alleged migraines. This is not completely true, and as stated is untrue. I have stated to you on the phone that I am willing to stop smoking cigarettes if you will sign a statement agreeing to allow me to take necessary prescription medications to cure the migraines. Taking nothing is not an option as my general physician has stated that it is a hazard to my health.

**5)** Please do not contact me other than e-mail. Please do not contact my workplace, my friends or any relatives past or present. Defamation of character and slander is a crime.

**6)** It states that you will pay the surrogate the surrogate fee (which now needs to be adjusted due to the change in doctors) minus the $1500. I am sending you this letter and a check for $1500 (to repay this first payment) as well as the other $500 you requested to repay you for the gas money, food, etc. Please do not send me any further finances including maternity clothing allowance at 12 weeks gestation. Any further finances can be paid at time of birth or completion of DNA testing upon confirmation of paternity. In other words, I do not want any money from you until after confirmation of paternity whatsoever. Contact must be limited to e-mail or USPS mail effective immediately.

I am sending this letter and the check, as stated above, via certified mail.

When we received this e-mail we thought, this woman is crazy. She is angry at us because we are concerned about our baby! At first Jennifer was saying she only smoked occasionally to help with her migraines; and then she said she smoked regularly throughout her entire pregnancies with her two biological children. And now we were back to her saying that she only smoked for her migraine headaches, which were supposedly more dangerous than smoking. We were thinking that no midwife or doctor would give a pregnant woman permission to smoke cigarettes while pregnant. The Surgeon General's report on women and smoking lists a number of risks for babies whose mothers smoke cigarettes while pregnant.

And if Jennifer did smoke, why would she smoke at our home and risk getting caught smoking unless she wanted to get caught? So many things were going through our minds at the time this transpired. Things didn't add up.

Over the course of several weeks, we sent a number of e-mails to Jennifer that went unanswered. This was one of several of those e-mail messages we sent to her:

Jennifer, I don't want to make this a war. We can either work this out or get a mediator. If we have to get a mediator we would have to go half and half on the cost per the contract and I know you said you're on a tight budget. I didn't send the [Breach of Contract] letter to be irritating to you. I was only following what you had written in the contract to do when a breach of contract was made. We can work this out thru e-mails and that way you don't have to talk to me if you wish. And for the record, I never gave you an amount or asked you to pay me for food, gas, etc. So if you send me a check I won't cash it. I didn't want any money as I stated before and that $500 amount you came up with, not me. All [we] have been doing is following procedures. Just remember you won't ever have to see us again, you only need to e-mail us to let us know when your doctor's visits are so we can get a progress report on the baby and how it is doing. We only have 5 and a 1/2 months to get thru this and be civil for the baby's sake and it's all over. I promise to never burden you again. So let me know what you would like to do.

At this point we were still trying to work things out and save this surrogacy. When Jennifer never responded to any of our e-mails, I knew that she had no intention of working this out. I tried to tell my husband this was a scam and her intentions were clear. But Tom was in denial that someone could use their own child to scam someone.

After several weeks went by, we finally received an e-mail from Jennifer and this was her response:

Tom and Gwen [sic]:

Upon last correspondence, you requested an amniocentesis to be done to determine paternity. I have scheduled such through the following company

[name of company]

[address of company in Jacksonville]

The cost for the actual procedure is $1400. You need to arrange payment prior to my scheduled appointment, Monday, November 27, 2006.

Furthermore, you also need to give your sample at the following location:

[name and address of hospital]

Prior to going, you will need to contact Mark ... to schedule this appointment and he can arrange the necessary kits being available and how it will go to the lab.

The lab costs for the test will cost $450. Again, when you speak with Mark, you can arrange this payment.

You must arrange payment and have your part of the paternity test complete prior to my scheduled appointment or my appointment will be cancelled [sic]. Due to my schedule, I will be unable to reschedule another appointment until after the holidays.

Our response to this e-mail:

An as far as the DNA test I will have to do it after the holidays, as I will be out of town. When you schedule your next appointment you will need to give me more notice, a two week notice, so I can work it in to my schedule since I have to go out of town for work.

Jennifer came back with this response to our e-mail:

I have rescheduled my appointment for Dec. 22. You can call Mark [phone number] to schedule YOUR appointment at the address below in a prior e-mail for anytime between now and Dec. 21. Your sample will hold "good" for awhile, so you can give yours anytime. You will also need to make arrangements for payments prior to 12/21 as well.

This is the e-mail that my husband wrote November 23, 2006, to the surrogate, which was also documented in court records. Jennifer's lawyers later took this out of context and threw it in our faces:

Gwyn wants me to do the test and she wants the baby. On the other hand I don't. I want to end this here and now. So I will need time to work this out. It may take a week or months I don't know. I will let you know once I do.

This note was sent by Tom without my knowledge. You see, at this point Tom was so frustrated with knowing that Jennifer had all the cards and we had no say in anything. My husband sent this message before any DNA test was done, and he was under the impression from Jennifer that this might not even be his baby.

As stated in court records, Tom was under the impression that Jennifer was having affairs while doing this surrogacy. At least that is what she had led him to believe. Of course, he did not want a child that was not even his. A letter from Jennifer's own attorney proved what Tom was saying was true.

This letter was not entered into evidence because of our inadequate counsel. If it had been, this document would have proved to the judge and everyone else that we did indeed want this child, but only if it was proven by DNA to be biologically related to my husband. This letter from Jennifer's attorney was verified by ABC News and will be noted in the next chapter.

# Chapter 4

# The Surrogate
# Gets an Attorney

$O$ne week later we received our first call from Jennifer's attorney. We let him know we were quite irritated with Jennifer's attitude. We told him at that time that Jennifer had given us reason to believe this baby was not ours.

The attorney responded that there was no contract; no contract existed. This is the letter sent to us from her attorney, verifying what we told him about wanting the child – *if* it was ours.

December 7, 2006

Dear Mr. Lamintina [sic]:

Thank you for speaking with me regarding your current involvement with my client, [the surrogate]. This letter will memorialize our conversation.

As we discussed, my client has suggested you have challenged the paternity of the child she currently carries. You have suggested that if this is your child you would like to take custody of it upon birth. You also suggested that if this is not your child you are not interested in being involved with the child. To clarify this issue a paternity test is required. As the child is not born this test will involve a surgical procedure. My client has verified that she has scheduled this test and made you aware of the timing and costs involved. You responded that you are not available. It is my understanding of this procedure that your involvement is minimal and that collection of your genetic sample can be accomplished through contracted medical service professionals wherever you may be at the time. As such I hereby request you contact this office regarding your availability and whereabouts to accomplish this goal.

Another issue is the cost involved. As a participant we hereby request you contribute 1/2 of the costs involved and, if your paternity is established, ask that you reimburse the other 1/2 of the costs at that time. These costs have been confirmed from the lab – [lab name and address] – and a formal invoice can be provided directly from the lab following the procedure. It is unclear whether this quoted cost is simply for the procedure to be performed on my client only, or inclusive of your test as well. Regardless, we request 1/2 of the total amount.

We also discussed your willingness to proceed if you are the genetic parent. You referenced a contract which you believe controls the issue. I have not been able to verify that a contract exists in this matter. Please be aware that my client contends that there is no contract. As such, if your paternity is established, we will need to proceed with drafting a contract to control the future relationship between yourself and my client. I highly recommend you seek the advise [sic] of counsel in this matter and forward my information to your lawyer for future negotiations.

In the meantime, please contact my office regarding your availability of the genetic test. This is necessary to understand which issues must be addressed. As you can see time is of the essence as my client continues to develop this child and it will arrive regardless of our scheduling. Please contact me to make arrangements as soon as possible to avoid unnecessary litigation and legal procedures.

Should you have any questions regarding the foregoing, please do not hesitate to contact me.

This letter finally proved to Tom what I had been trying to tell him: Jennifer had planned this all along. It was a scam. If you looked back at Jennifer's response to the Breach of Contract letter, paragraph two, Jennifer mentioned the original contract. Not only that, but she was holding us to the traditional surrogacy contract by mentioning her compensation fee.

We knew that Jennifer had cashed our first payment for the surrogacy, so we were thinking at this point that whether she signed the contract or not, she made this a binding contract because she took proceeds from it. We thought it was basic contract law. On top of that, we had proof she was referring to the traditional surrogacy contract throughout the Breach of Contract response that she sent us.

Since Jennifer faxed us the signature page for the traditional surrogacy contract over the Internet with her name and home phone number on it, we had her for federal fraud, because it was sent by fax. So now we not only had the fax, but the e-mailed Breach of Contract response and the letter sent to us by her attorney, claiming that no contract existed.

We thought we had Jennifer for e-mail fraud, extortion for cashing the check and then trying to negotiate for more money from us, and mail fraud because her attorney sent us a letter stating there was no contract and a contract needed to be drafted to control the situation.

After receiving the letter from Jennifer's attorney, we talked to him over the phone and he stated again that no contract existed. Tom told the attorney that yes; the traditional surrogacy contract did exist because Jennifer had cashed our check. And there was a signed contract because the midwife had it, or so Jennifer had told us. The attorney asked us why we didn't just send him a copy of the traditional surrogacy contract that we claimed existed. Tom told the attorney that he should have the surrogacy contract right in front of him, since his client certainly should have a copy; after all, she drafted it in the first place. Tom told Jennifer's attorney that if he wanted to see the traditional surrogacy contract, he could see it when we went to court.

After several harassing phone calls from this attorney trying to get Tom to do a DNA test when he was out of town on business, he tried to convince Tom that if he would just sign away his rights to the child, he wouldn't have to pay child support and this would all be over. I tried to tell Tom that even if he signed away his rights, it would not release him from his obligation to pay child support.

As all this was going on, we didn't even know if it was Tom's biological child. This seemed very suspect to me. But after constant harassment, Tom asked Jennifer's attorney to send the papers, just to get the man off his back and to prove what I had tried to tell him, that there would be no mention in the papers of a release from paying child support.

Jennifer's attorney must have thought we were stupid. After we received the papers from him to sign our rights away, we reported this to the police. They thought it was suspicious that an attorney would be sending us papers to sign away our rights in the first place – especially when no DNA test had been done and paternity had not been established.

I knew that they wanted Tom to sign away his rights to our child and then Jennifer and her attorney would come after us for child support. That way we would end up paying child support but not have any legal right to see the child or be involved in the child's life

At this time we decided to go ahead with this DNA test, because if the child was not my husband's biological child, this entire matter would be over. So we agreed that we would have my husband give his DNA sample to facilitate the testing, but we would not pay half the cost of doing the test as this child might not even be ours. We knew from Jennifer's track record that we would never get our money back if the DNA test came back negative.

So Tom went to get tested. He was indeed the father of this baby. That is when we found out it was a girl. Jennifer's attorney sounded almost giddy with excitement when he called my husband to tell us that Tom was the father of this child, that it was a girl, and that Jennifer had decided to keep her. I just knew that Jennifer had told her attorney that we were hoping for a girl. So Tom hung up the phone and we went to find an attorney of our own. Jennifer's attorney called back and Tom would not answer the call.

Jennifer's attorney sent us this letter, dated January 15, 2007:

Dear Mr. Lamitina:

This letter is to confirm that you are being represented by counsel, and you are hesitant to give us the name of your attorney. This office needs to be able to communicate with you. If you do not provide us with a name of your attorney, we will be forced to communicate directly with you. In the meantime, we will continue to contact you directly. Please send your attorney's information as soon as possible.

If you should have any questions regarding the foregoing, please do not hesitate to contact me.

Our attorney sent Jennifer's attorney a letter to say that we now had representation and all correspondence must be handled through her. Soon after our attorney sent this letter to Jennifer's attorney, both we and our attorney received a letter from Jennifer's attorney:

January 18, 2007

Dear [attorney's name]:

Thank you for your correspondence. We will forward all communications to your office.

Please forward a copy of the contract you allege that exists between your client, Mr. Lamitina and my client, [the surrogate].

Please be advised this case will be forwarded to another attorney as it has now become a child support issue.

In the meantime should you have any questions regarding the foregoing, please do not hesitate to contact me.

Why we would want to send the contract to Jennifer's attorney? We figured that she and her attorney either had the signed surrogacy contract, or they wanted to see if we had obtained a signed copy from the midwife or OB/GYN. And why was Jennifer's attorney now turning her case over to another attorney?

Maybe Jennifer's attorney couldn't handle cases that became custody issues. So as time went on, we began to have our attorney subpoena everything we thought would be beneficial to us in finding out if this woman really did sign the contract. We needed to know if this was fraud, as we suspected.

And we knew that if we wanted to get as much information as we could about this woman, we needed help. We discussed with our attorney the possibility of hiring an investigator to see what we could find out about Jennifer.

We did hire an investigator and he discovered that Jennifer's roommate Sue was listed on the mortgage with Jennifer as co-owner, as well as on the titles of their cars, bank accounts and credit cards. Furthermore, the investigator talked to Sue's ex-husband and found out that, contrary to what both Jennifer and Sue had told us, Sue never adopted Jennifer as her daughter. According to him, the two women met because Sue worked with special needs children, and had been working with Jennifer's oldest child.

When asked if the child that lived with Jennifer and Sue on whether or not that child was indeed Sue's biological child, he said that it was highly unlikely that this child was Sue's.

The investigator also looked into the story Jennifer had told us about a child bringing a loaded gun into her school. He checked it out with the school directly and found that it was not true. The school also informed the investigator that the conference that Jennifer claimed she had to attend that last weekend she came to our house was not related to her job. A school representative said that they would not send one of their teachers to a conference that far away; their conferences for teachers are held locally, in Jacksonville. This was more confirmation for us that this was a set-up planned by Jennifer and Sue.

While we were getting information about Jennifer, our attorney explained to us that there was not much that we could do legally until the baby was born. It was going to be a waiting game for several months, but in the meantime we would gather as much information about these people as we could.

# Chapter 5

# Time For the Media

$A$s the date for the baby's birth approached, Tom and I discussed going to the media as another way to get our story out there, and see if that would generate new information about Jennifer. Could Jennifer possibly have done this to someone else, or were we the first? We had hired an investigator early on in our case but didn't get very far.

The media would enable us to get this story out to more people at one time and we needed that advantage. We just knew someone would come forward with useful information. If we only had known just how many people were going to come forward about this woman we would have done it earlier. To be honest, I was not happy about going to the press at all. Our privacy would be violated, and I knew how things like that can come back to bite you.

But I also knew we could not let this happen to someone else. That was our main motivation, and we wanted to obtain information that would help us get our little girl and prove that what we had suspected was true – even if it meant that some people wouldn't understand. We had a feeling that there was someone out there that had known this surrogate and had dealings with her that were similar to ours. It seemed that Jennifer knew all too well what she was doing.

We started calling local media outlets to see if they would be interested in our story. The response was that if this was just another story about a surrogate changing her mind, they weren't interested. But if it was something else, backed up with paperwork, they would air it. So we began to send them all the paperwork we had. Tom followed up with a reporter, who agreed that it looked like we had been scammed.

The reporter scheduled a time for us to come to the local television studio for an interview. Shortly after that we found out that the child had been born. No one had bothered to call us to inform us that our daughter had been born. The child was almost two weeks old by this time. Not only did we have to find this out through the media, but it was shortly after that Jennifer's attorney served us with papers. We were going to court.

In the meantime, we decided that we would call our health insurance provider to get ready to add our daughter to our policy. We set up an appointment for the insurance agent to come to our home to fill out the paperwork.

The insurance agent arrived, along with a new agent in training. We explained that we wanted to add our daughter to the policy. The agent looked around and asked us where our daughter was. We explained the situation to the agent.

As we told the insurance agent our story and the name of the surrogate, the agent told us that the name sounded familiar. The agent went on to describe what she thought Jennifer looked like. She asked us if Jennifer had short brown hair, brown eyes, was tall, skinny, flat-chested – and did she act a little strange.

The agent's description of Jennifer was right on, even to the point that she remembered that Jennifer did something odd with her hands. Tom and I looked at each other and just knew that this had to be our surrogate. Jennifer had an uncontrollable tick: she would nervously rub her hands together.

This was unbelievable. What were the odds that this insurance agent would know Jennifer? The agent went on to tell us that she remembered Jennifer talking about doing surrogacies and how she was going to make $30,000 per surrogacy and that she could even smoke while pregnant.

We asked the agent where she met Jennifer. She told us that she met Jennifer while she was bartending at a gentlemen's club and that Jennifer was one of the strippers. And she said that Jennifer went by a stage name.

We asked her if she remembered the name that Jennifer used while working as a stripper. When we heard it you could have knocked us over with a feather. It was the same name that Jennifer had named our daughter.

While the insurance lady was at our home we showed her a picture of Jennifer that had been shown on the local media stations of her as she was leaving her home. We wanted to make sure Jennifer was indeed the same person that the insurance lady had described. But she said that the picture did not show Jennifer's face good enough for her to say that she was definitely the one that worked at the strip club.

We began to put things together and remembered that the private investigator we had hired early on in this case had mentioned to us that he couldn't figure out how Jennifer was making enough money to pay her bills. At this point in time Jennifer did not have a job outside the home and had been watching a couple of children in her home to make some money.

This in-home daycare Jennifer was running out of her home would not bring in enough money by itself for her to pay her bills. We knew that Jennifer had told us that we couldn't call her after 8 p.m. because she always was in bed by that time.

So was Jennifer going to bed, or was the she going to her other job? This had to be divine intervention from the Lord. What were the chances we would run into an insurance agent who knew Jennifer?

The more times we were on the news telling our story, the more people came forward about Jennifer and the strangeness surrounding her, her roommate Sue, and their actions. One woman, who had blogged on one of the surrogacy forums, wrote that she and her husband had done a traditional surrogacy and exactly the same thing happened to them.

Not only that, but their surrogate and Jennifer attended the same high school and had followed the same script. Of course that sounded very interesting, so we contacted this intended mother and she filled us in with quite a bit of information. We began to think were we right – this could be a conspiracy. Other intended parents were experiencing the same situation.

Perhaps this was the scenario that some surrogates (and I hesitate to call them surrogates) were following. Soon after pregnancy is confirmed, the surrogate purposely breaches the contract and/or says she did not sign the contract, knowing from the beginning of the surrogacy that she will not give up the baby. The surrogate then cashes in on 18 years of child support and other financial assistance. It was starting to look that way.

We could not believe the stories that started to come to our attention and we began to think this could be a serious conspiracy. Could we be uncovering other scams with other intended parents like us who these surrogates were preying on? Were we naive enough to think that we could have been the first to be scammed in a surrogacy? We didn't think so. And if we were not the first couple this had happened to, did this same type of scenario play out across the United States, maybe even around the world? It was too hard to wrap our minds around.

As our story came out, we began to see similar stories across the United States, as well as other countries, indicating it was definitely not just us being duped in this despicable way. Someone had found a loophole in the laws dealing with surrogacies and was utilizing it to the fullest. We had no idea what we were getting ourselves into. But we knew one thing – if we didn't take a stand now, this could continue to happen. Preventing this tragedy from happening to other couples drove us to keep this story in the public eye.

Through more investigation and consultation with our first surrogate, we discovered more inconsistencies surrounding Jennifer. You see, our first surrogate was very experienced. She had done six egg donations and two surrogacies, one gestational and one traditional; and she had started her own surrogacy agency.

This agency was to match intended parents and surrogates together to give parents unable to conceive a child a safer way to find compatible surrogates. When we told our first surrogate about Jennifer's online ad, she knew immediately we were being set up.

The first suspicious thing she pointed out to us was that Jennifer had put in her ad that she had done three egg donations and a gestational surrogacy, and had now become allergic to the medications required to do a gestational surrogacy.

I had asked Jennifer on our first meeting in Jacksonville if she would do a gestational surrogacy for us, because we had frozen eggs from our previous surrogacy. Jennifer had explained that she had become allergic to the medications required to do a gestational surrogacy.

Our first surrogate said that this should have raised red flags from the start. She explained that when doing egg donations or a gestational surrogacy, synthetic hormones need to be injected. When you do egg donations, you take even more of these hormones than when doing a gestational surrogacy, because you are trying to produce more eggs than you would normally produce in a regular menstrual cycle.

The hormones injected during a gestational surrogacy are hormones that the body produces naturally, such as estrogen and progesterone. The likelihood of being allergic to these hormones is very slim. Even if there was the chance that a surrogate might be allergic to one particular drug, several other medications could be used.

Had Jennifer been willing to do a gestational surrogacy like we wanted to do in the first place, we would have been protected by state laws. In Florida, a surrogate doing a gestational surrogacy would not have any rights to the child. The surrogate in a gestational surrogacy has no biological relationship to the child; therefore the child would go directly to the intended parents after the child was born. We were thinking, how much more suspect can this story get?

We were beginning to think that Jennifer probably never even did egg donations or a gestational surrogacy as she claimed in her ad, and that she was trying to look more experienced as a surrogate than she really was. And there was also the third child living with Jennifer and Sue. This third child seemed to us to be more attached to Jennifer than to Sue, the alleged biological mother.

And when we began to investigate this third child, we discovered that Jennifer and Sue, who lived in Duval County, had gone to Ft. Meyers in Lee County to do an adoption proceeding for the gestational surrogacy that Jennifer had allegedly done for Sue.

Why, first of all, would they go 300 miles to do an adoption in Lee County they could have easily done in Jacksonville, where they lived? Any adoption attorney could have handled an adoption of this nature if this was a gestational surrogacy as Jennifer claimed.

Second, our attorney said that this adoption should have taken place within three days of the child's birth. Why would they wait 13 months to perform this adoption? This was just another suspicious activity involving Jennifer and Sue, more indication that maybe this third child was actually Jennifer's.

And perhaps the reason the adoption was delayed was because Jennifer was fighting with the intended parents of this third child the same way she had been fighting with us. Perhaps it took 13 months before the other intended parents finally gave up. We thought this third child who Jennifer kept could be the result of another traditional surrogacy gone bad.

We had so much information indicating that this could be nothing but a scam. Some of the evidence was circumstantial, but we were so close to exposing this woman. All the information we were getting about Jennifer kept pointing us to this third child who lived with her and Sue.

I knew Sue would have been around 41 years old when she did this gestational surrogacy with Jennifer. I knew from my experience with fertility clinics that, in most cases, they would not extract eggs from a woman over 35.

What I had learned dealing with fertility clinics was that the older a woman is, the less chance that any extracted eggs would be viable eggs that could be used to get a surrogate pregnant. And the number of eggs that could be extracted or produced would be much less than in a younger woman.

In most cases, this procedure would likely have to be performed several times before the surrogate became pregnant. So the cost could become astronomical. Usually the clinic would insert at least two embryos, sometimes three, depending on the clinic.

If the embryos did not take and the surrogate did not get pregnant, and if the older mother who had donated her eggs was lucky enough to have more embryos frozen, the intended mother might get another try. And, hopefully, without going through another series of taking hormone shots and starting over from scratch. You can see why most clinics were not in favor of taking women over the age of 35 due to potential costs and complications.

Depending on the location, a gestational surrogacy could easily cost intended parents $30,000 per attempt, and that's in addition to the surrogate's fee. That figure does not cover the cost of drugs or hormones that are to be taken by both the intended mother and the surrogate, and it does not cover the fee to transfer the embryos to the surrogate mother. You can see how expensive this type of surrogacy could get for intended parents.

Sue, for whom Jennifer claimed to have done a gestational surrogacy, had previously been married for quite some time and had never had any children during this marriage. If Sue had wanted children, why did she wait until she was unmarried and 41?

Early on, when the investigator talked to Sue's ex-husband, he had indicated to the investigator that this third child being Sue's was highly unlikely. We knew in our gut that there was more to this story. We needed to find out whether this was truly a gestational surrogacy or not.

After receiving the court documents for the adoption that was performed by Jennifer and Sue in Lee County, our attorney called the attorney who was hired to handle this proceeding. Of course that attorney could not divulge any information surrounding the case, but he was able to tell us that the two women knew *exactly* what they wanted.

We also found out that a sperm donor's name was mentioned in the court documents. That seemed strange to us and our attorney because normally when two single women go into a clinic to do a gestational surrogacy, an anonymous sperm donor is used. So this person named on the documents must have been someone they knew.

If this sperm donor was someone Jennifer and Sue knew, the clinic should have made sure in any case that the sperm donor had signed his rights away before the sperm was even donated, to protect him from possibly being sued later for child support. This was a requirement of Florida law told to us by our attorney, that all sperm donors, whether anonymous or not, had to comply with before donating their sperm to a clinic. This was also the same information given to us by the clinic we had dealt with previously.

So it struck us as odd that the sperm donor would wait until 13 months after the child was born to give up his rights to the child. In fact, there should have been no mention of the sperm donor's name in the adoption proceedings unless this sperm donor was actually the intended father in a traditional surrogacy, and this intended father thought he had no other choice. Could this sperm donor have been fighting this surrogate just as we were, trying to get his child, and finally felt like he had no choice but to give in?

We knew how that could have happened; we had thought many times the same thing, that should we give up, and give in. The law was definitely not on the side of the intended parents, especially in the situation we found ourselves in. Time after time we had seen intended parents paying child support, life insurance and health insurance to surrogates and they didn't even get to see the child.

Soon after going to the media we found out that Jennifer and her attorney had actually filed against us first and we were served with papers. We were to appear in court to decide custody issues, such as how much money my husband was going to pay for child support, health insurance and life insurance with Jennifer as the beneficiary.

And not only that, but Jennifer wanted our rights as parents to be terminated. We couldn't believe it. This woman had some nerve to think she could get child support and everything else she wanted and then terminate our rights to see the child.

How this could be possible? Could this actually happen? Wasn't the court supposed to look out for the best interests of the child? We had hoped that the judicial system was going to work. We may have not had a legal contract as far as the surrogacy went, but we had a contract all the same. Jennifer took monies from the proceeds of this contract and thus ratified the contract and made the contract binding. At least that was what our attorney was telling us.

Through our attorney we started to subpoena everything we thought would be pertinent to our case. But of course, Jennifer's lawyers fought every subpoena. We finally were supposed to get an emergency hearing to try for temporary custody. This process took two months.

Well, if a two-month wait was getting an "emergency" hearing, we certainly didn't believe it. We finally got a court date and a time. We were excited! We thought if we could just get temporary custody until permanent custody was established, at least we could have our baby girl with us and enjoy time with her.

The attorneys kept us away from our daughter and we had not been allowed even to see the baby. We were not even informed of her birth.

Tom contacted Vital Statistics to obtain a birth certificate for our baby. Even with a DNA test showing proof positive that he was the father of the child, Vital Statistics would not send us a copy of the birth certificate. We were devastated to find out that not only were we being denied access to our little girl, but now we were not even able to obtain a birth certificate. And to top it all off, Jennifer had not put Tom on the birth certificate as being the father.

We were having our hearts ripped out. And the worst part was that our little girl was the real victim. She didn't deserve any of this. This little girl had the right to both a mother and a father. We had tried diligently to work this out with Jennifer before all of this got out of hand, before the attorneys were hired. We were willing to go to a third party, a mediator, to sit down and discuss a better option, but to no avail; all fell on deaf ears.

I started doing my own research, checking out other high profile cases such as the Baby M case. In most cases such as ours, with the exception of the Baby M case, the intended parents lost custody and if they got to see the child it was only part time.

It seemed no matter what, in divorces that involve child custody or in cases of our type, the mother always won out. You had to prove the mother unfit for the court not to rule in her favor.

We were getting more and more frustrated. But our attorney kept telling us we had a good case, that even though Jennifer had not signed the contract, we had proof that she took money or proceeds from the contract which in turn made the contract binding. But we would soon find out that even that is up to interpretation. How could this not be a binding contract? Basic law, right? We even had evidence of Jennifer trying to renegotiate the terms of the contract.

We wondered how much more proof would we need, with or without Jennifer's signature on a contract. Jennifer was trying to get even more money out of us because of the embarrassment she had caused herself. Jennifer said she could no longer have a home birth and was going to have to give birth in the hospital; therefore it was going to cost us more money.

This was incredible that someone could be doing this to her own child. All we wanted was to get our baby girl, as originally agreed. Up until Jennifer got her attorney and we had to get ours, we were telling her we would still pay the surrogacy fee as long as she would sign the baby girl over to us when the child was born.

But we kept thinking to ourselves that Jennifer wanted more than just her surrogacy fee. This was made painfully obvious when she filed the lawsuit against us first. And we knew because of the strange and deceptive behavior that was going on throughout this surrogacy relationship – and especially the bizarre behavior that last weekend we saw Jennifer at our house – we were being set up.

We thought that the laws Florida had in place for surrogacies would help us. And we just knew that Jennifer's health care provider had to have a signed contract before they could give her medical care.

We thought for sure that we would just subpoena the midwife and Jennifer's OB/GYN and find a signed contract. When doing our previous surrogacy, both the clinic and the OB/GYN that gave our previous surrogate medical care would not even see her without a signed surrogacy contract.

So we thought we were going to find a signed contract, and that Jennifer would be forced to comply with the contract and give up custody of the baby to us. At the time, we were not even opposed to her seeing the child whenever she was able to do so.

We never intended for Jennifer not to ever see the child. A child needs to have loving people around her. It takes a village, so to speak, to raise a child. So we were not opposed to her seeing the child, yet she wanted us to have no connection, no parental rights to this child whatsoever.

In her complaint against us, Jennifer even hinted that we were unfit to have this child. As if we were terrible parents. Jennifer didn't seem to think so when she agreed to do this surrogacy and even up until the pregnancy. What had changed now? If we were bad parents as Jennifer claimed, why had she not ended this relationship with us long before? She claimed in court that we would not be loving parents. Well, anybody with any sense could look at our son and see that he was loved, and it was obvious to anybody who knew us personally, too.

We could tell Jennifer was going to play dirty. If this woman was going after us for the money, that was not a very smart decision. If we did have money, then we could, and would, fight her tooth-and-nail for this child. We could afford the best attorneys, but we were far from being rich. In fact, the equity loan we took out on our house was in part to pay Jennifer her fee for this surrogacy. We were now using the surrogacy money to pay for our attorney fees – and it was going quick.

Several months later the housing market plummeted in Florida. Tom's job in construction would come to a screeching halt as well. We were using all the resources we had to borrow the money to continue our fight. Thank God for Tom's mother, who helped us so much financially throughout this case.

We were now on our second attorney and we were finding it difficult to find one who wanted to include us in the decisions that he was making on our case. These attorneys wanted to what we called "John Wayne" our case – do everything without any input from us. We couldn't even get these people to keep us updated and informed on our case. Here we were, getting ready to have this hearing on July 31, to see if we even had a case to go to court.

We were riding an emotional roller coaster. Tom and I would soon realize that even after being together for 18 years, this would definitely test our relationship. At times we wondered how much longer our relationship could endure so much stress.

We knew if we could make it through this and keep our marriage intact and our love for each other alive, at the end we would be rewarded with a much deeper and closer relationship. But it wasn't easy, and to add insult to injury, our attorney indicated that the judge assigned to our case was not the best one we could have going into this hearing.

Boy, we didn't even know the half of it. As the date of the hearing approached, I became more and more apprehensive. I just didn't have a good feeling about the judge and how our attorneys were handling our case, but we were praying and leaving this in God's hands. My husband felt confident that we were going to win. In fact, Tom was much more positive and had such a good feeling about how this was going to turn out when we went to court.

We fell back on our faith in God to give us the strength to get through such a trying time in our lives. We had never needed an attorney before; this was all new to us and we made a lot of mistakes. We had to trust an attorney with our lives and the life of our child. That was not an easy decision to make.

We pretty much experienced every emotion possible. We felt so helpless and all these lawyers wanted us to put our daughter and our lives in their hands. At the end of the day they went home to life as usual, but the same could not be said about us. I will be honest – we just didn't like attorneys and it seemed that every time we changed attorneys that feeling was reinforced. To them, this was just another case.

We just did not have confidence in their ability to win this case, and each time we were proven right. This was a real test of our faith in God and we wondered at times if God was hearing our prayers. And yet things happened during this case that no one could explain for example, the insurance agent who came to our house and just happened to have known Jennifer.

On one particular occasion we were feeling pretty low and it was one of those times when we all wonder if God is listening, if God really cares. We had been praying hard for some kind of sign, any sign at all that God was listening.

We were on our way back from Tom's mother's house and something caught my attention up in the sky. I looked up and I saw a plane skywriting something. At first I thought maybe someone was proposing to someone and had hired the pilot to write the proposal in the sky.

Without even realizing it, I began to speak out loud the letters being spelled out by the plane. When I saw what was being written I started to cry. I think Tom at first thought I was losing my mind, but as I spelled out the letters to him, he too saw what was happening.

We both stared at each other with tears streaming down our faces. The message said: Jesus Loves You. Was this God's way of letting us know he was hearing our prayers and letting us know he was with us? There was no doubt in our minds.

You could say it was a coincidence, but we know in our hearts that it was our confirmation that God does hear prayers, that God does care about your situation. That was just one of the many times that we got confirmation of our prayers and faith being answered.

Two weeks before the first hearing was to be held at the end of July, we hired yet another attorney. Each attorney promised he would do specific things in our case, that we definitely had a good case, promised to do what it took to win, etc. Each one was good at telling us what they were going to do – but not so good at coming through on their promises.

At this point we were running out of money. Each attorney we hired wanted a $5,000 to $7,000 retainer just to get started. Let me tell you, those retainers didn't last long. We didn't know how much longer we could keep up the fight.

The business that Tom started years before started to slow down. We were on rocky ground, not just emotionally but financially. We were approaching very quickly the one-year point in the fight for our daughter.

Every time we thought about giving up we only had to look at our son and realize had this been him we were fighting for, we would have fought as long as we could possibly fight. We knew that we could not live with ourselves if our daughter came up to us years later and said, "Why didn't you fight for me? Didn't you care?"

We were going broke, even close to losing our home at times. Nobody could have blamed us if we had given up. But we knew in our hearts that this woman had taken advantage of us. New legislation and better laws were needed to protect intended parents as well as surrogates.

We wanted to protect others doing a surrogacy after us and ensure a good experience for intended parents as well as surrogates involved in traditional surrogacy. We knew from experience that this method of having children could be a good thing.

We had done it successfully, it could work, but there had to be better legislation in place to protect the families and the surrogates that would take away any chance of someone taking advantage of the loopholes in the surrogacy law. Both families and surrogates needed a source of information before entering into a surrogacy, to see if this was the right thing for them.

We would never advise someone not to do a surrogacy, even now. For us to tell anyone not to do a traditional surrogacy would discount that we have a beautiful son we could not have had otherwise. Every time we look at him, we know that we made the right choice for us.

While we were waiting for the hearing that was scheduled at the end of July, we were contacted by Fox News. Fox sent our story to New York and we were getting calls to be guests on *The O'Reilly Factor*. This story had gone national. We thought we were going to get the exposure needed to get more information to help us with our case.

More people would see this interview and hopefully we could stop this from happening again and maybe get some information from someone who knew Jennifer and had dealings with her before. But our new attorney had only had our case one day – he was not ready to discuss our case on television just yet.

After our attorney had familiarized himself with our case, we had him appear on *The O'Reilly Factor*. Up to this point, we were the only ones who had been going on television talking about our case. So it was nice that we finally had an attorney who would go on television and answer questions. It made what we were saying all along about this case more credible.

This attorney wasn't scared of the press. In fact, he became somewhat of a media hog and why not? His law practice was getting the type of attention money can't buy.

The day before the hearing we were getting ready to go up to Jacksonville. We had planned to stay at a motel close to the courthouse. This way we wouldn't have to wake up so early in the morning to get to the courthouse by 10 a.m. The drive for us from Orlando to Jacksonville was a good two-

and-one-half hours one way. Tom was so excited – he just knew we were going to be bringing home our little girl. She was already just over two months old.

He was so excited that he had already installed the baby car seat in the back seat next to our son's, just so we would be ready to bring home our baby. I was trying to be positive but I felt deep down that this was not going to be as simple as Tom thought. I kept my feelings to myself so as not to burst his bubble. He was so positive we were going to win this case. I was not feeling as confident about the legal system as he was.

We got up the next day and headed to the courthouse. We knew the press would be there. The judge would not allow the media into the hearing, but we knew they would be waiting outside.

# Chapter 6

# The One-Hour Hearing

$A$s we entered the courthouse we had to pass through officers and security. I became separated from Tom, who went on up to the hearing without me. When I finally was able to get up to the second floor of the courthouse to the judge's chambers, the hearing had begun and everyone, including the media and the witnesses, was sitting in the hallway outside the judge's chambers.

I went in to talk to the judge's assistant to get into the hearing with Tom. But I was told I was not on the list of persons that were to be in the judge's chambers. I was shocked that my name wasn't on the list. But there was no use in trying to convince the judge's assistant; she was not going to let me go in with Tom and our attorney.

I was asked to sit outside in the hallway until my name was called. When I stepped back out into the hallway, the reporters were shocked when I told them that I was not allowed to be a part of the hearing.

Everyone expected the hearing to take three hours but it only lasted one. The first person to come out after the hearing was Tom and he looked dumbfounded.

I asked him immediately what was going on, was everything okay? By this time, the media had swarmed around Tom, sticking microphones in his face. One of the reporters noticed I was being left out, and asked the others to let me through to get to my husband's side.

Tom began to tell the media that he was shocked that Jennifer had confessed the existence of a contract and that she took the money for this contract, which made the contract binding. Not only that, she admitted that she tried to get more money out of us.

Jennifer had, in her response to our Breach of Contract letter, informed us that she was going to be changing doctors, and that she would be giving birth in a hospital. However, in this proceeding, in front of the judge, Jennifer admitted that she had not changed doctors and that she had the baby at home, delivered by a midwife.

When our attorney questioned Jennifer on this statement about whether she was trying to get more money out of us by telling us she was having the baby in the hospital, she admitted that she was.

To say we were shocked about Jennifer's admissions was an understatement. We thought there was no way this judge was going to let her keep our child. Jennifer's position all along had been that there was no contract.

The press asked Tom if the judge was going to render his decision that day. Tom told them that the judge had said he would consider all the evidence and information he had been presented with, but would not be making a decision on the case today.

The judge had another hearing scheduled and would let us know as soon as possible. My husband was disappointed that we didn't get our baby girl, but he was confident the judge would see it our way. As we finished up our conference with the media, Jennifer and her attorneys came out of the judge's chambers. The press tried to get her to make a comment on camera.

But Jennifer only smiled and kept walking. I noticed as she walked out of the judge's chambers that Jennifer did not look like herself, definitely not like the woman that Tom and I remembered. I commented that she looked pale, her face was heavily broken out, and her eyes were bulging somewhat.

Someone from the media overheard me say this about Jennifer's appearance, and asked me had she not looked like this all along. I told them no. The media asked us to keep them informed and to let them know as soon as the judge rendered a decision.

It was at this time that Jennifer's attorneys got the attention of the media and stated that they wanted to make a comment on camera. Our attorney wanted us to walk over and listen to what the surrogate's attorneys had to say. These attorneys told the press that my husband had sent an e-mail stating that he did not want the child.

Well, of course the media was all over that because they thought it was the first time they had heard this statement. But our attorney was quick to point out to the media that they had been given this e-mail earlier and it had been in their possession with all the other paperwork we had given to them. We had not tried to hide anything.

We had explained the reason for Tom sending this e-mail to Jennifer: she had given my husband reason to believe this child might not have been his biological child. We also pointed out to the media that we gave them a letter from Jennifer's attorneys verifying what we were saying was true.

This letter, dated December 7, said if the child was our biological child, we want it; if not, we didn't. Of course Jennifer's attorneys were trying to take what we said in the e-mail out of context.

Jennifer's attorneys went on to say to the media that Jennifer was the biological mother of this child and had the right to keep this child. After her attorneys were done with their statement to the media, the media asked us if they could meet us in Jacksonville on the day we were to pick up our daughter. The media felt confident as did we that the judge was going to see this case the way we did and give us custody of our daughter and they wanted to film us that day picking her up and taking her home. We agreed.

Before we went home, our attorney suggested that while we were in the Jacksonville area we should try to see the baby. But our attorney wanted to make sure that we took someone with us, such as a police officer, as a witness in case Jennifer tried to say something happened that didn't.

So Tom called Jennifer and left a message explaining that we would like to come by and see the baby. She didn't return our call, not that we thought she would. Our attorney suggested we take a chance and go to Jennifer's house anyway.

We headed over to the neighborhood where Jennifer lived and stopped at a convenience store just outside the subdivision to call for a police officer to assist us. The responding officers decided that they would go to the house first to scope out the situation and if everything was okay they would come back and escort us to Jennifer's home.

Before the police officers left, they asked my husband for his driver's license for identification to show to Jennifer. We waited at the convenience store for what seemed like forever. But when the officers returned they told us that Jennifer had refused to let us see the child; we would just have to wait until the trial was over and see what happened.

We were so disappointed. We wanted to see the baby, especially after Jennifer's attorneys had thrown in my husband's face the fact that he had never tried to come and see the child since she had been born. But we knew that Jennifer wouldn't let us see this child now or before this hearing; it was a ploy to make us look bad to the judge. So as we headed home we talked about some of the things that went on during the hearing.

One of the things that stuck out in my mind was when Tom mentioned the fact that the judge said that Tom had a long way to go to prove he was a father. I did not like the sound of that at all. I was thinking that this sounded like confirmation that the judge had already made up his mind that he wasn't planning on giving us custody of the child.

I asked Tom, what do we have to prove? He was the biological father. Did the judge mean that because my husband was not there monetarily and physically that he had to prove he was a father? It was not like we had a choice in the matter. Our attorney had contacted Jennifer's attorneys on many occasions throughout the pregnancy requesting medical information about the child, but Jennifer's attorneys would not allow us access to any of the health records for the child, much less, let us see the child. Neither Jennifer nor her attorneys even contacted us to tell us the baby was born. How can you be a father to a child you're being kept from?

After a long wait for the judge's decision, we got a call from a woman who worked with our attorney. This woman was the public relations person for the firm and had become a friend.

She told us she had e-mailed us with the judge's decision from the hearing. Of course we wanted to know the decision right away; she told us it wasn't bad, but it wasn't exactly what we wanted either, and we should read the e-mail and call her back if we had any questions. Tom couldn't believe that the judge did not give us temporary custody of our baby girl, but I wasn't surprised. I was truly hoping for the best and hoping that we would at least get a chance to see the child, but it was not meant to be. The judge did say that he wanted to hear more evidence and scheduled our trial for September 12.

Here is the judge's response to our hearing.

**Order Denying Second Emergency Motion for Custody and Visitation**

This cause came before the Court on July 31, 2007 on the Respondent's Second Emergency Motion for Custody and Visitation. The Court took testimony from the parties and received evidence. This case comes to the Court on the Petition for Determination of Paternity filed by [the surrogate], the birth mother. . . .

A. The testimony reveals that the Petitioner placed an online ad volunteering to act as a surrogate mother for the birth of a child. The Respondent responded to the online ad and the parties engaged in discussions concerning him providing sperm to impregnate her with a child. He testified that the Petitioner provided him with a written agreement which he signed and had his soon to be wife sign and returned it to the Petitioner for her signature.

He stated that she told him that she had received it and signed it and also that she would send him a copy but she never did. She testified she never signed the agreement. During the hearing, neither party had a copy of the agreement which was signed by the intended father and mother nor the surrogate. Counsel for the Respondent stated that he had a copy of the agreement signed by the Respondent and his soon to be wife and he asked to supplement the record by submitting that after the hearing. He has done so and the document which appears to be an identical copy of the unsigned document that was proffered during the hearing, with the addition to having the signatures of the Respondent and his soon to be wife, is marked as Respondent's Exhibit 4.

B. The intended parents signed the contract September 6, 2006. Apparently, at that time, the surrogate was already impregnated. The child was born May 9, 2007. During the pregnancy, the parties began to have disagreements. The intended father questioned whether he was actually the biological father of the child and requested a DNA test to confirm this. He also alleged that the surrogate was in material breach of the contract by smoking cigarettes and having unprotected sexual intercourse. She became concerned as to the father's moral and emotional stability. In October, 2006 the intended father communicated to the surrogate that he believed that she was in material breach of the contract. On November 23, 2006, he e-mailed her and stated "[my name] (intended mother) wants me to do the test and she wants the baby. On the other hand I don't. I want to end this here and now. So I will need time to work this out. It may take a week or months I don't know. I will let you know once I do." In January, 2007 she says she revoked and terminated the agreement.

C. In reviewing the Pre-Adoption Plan Contract, Respondent's Exhibit 4, the Court notes that there are several provisions that do not comply with 63.213, Fla. Stat. or are in contravention of that statue. Specifically, subsection (e) of the statute requires that the intended father and intended mother acknowledge that they may not receive custody or parental rights under the agreement if the volunteer mother terminates the agreement or if the volunteer mother terminates the agreement or if the volunteer mother rescinds her consent to place her child for adoption within 48 hours after birth. Subsection (i) states, "That the agreement may be terminated at any time by any of the parties." The contract provides in paragraph III(A)(6) "The Surrogate or the Intended Parents may withdraw their consent to this Agreement and may terminate this Agreement with written notice given to the other party anytime prior to conception by the Surrogate subject to the provisions provided below." In subparagraph (g) of the statute, it is provided "that the intended father and intended mother agree to accept custody of and to assert full parental rights and responsibilities for the child immediately upon the child's birth, regardless of any impairments of the child." The Pre-Adoption Plan Contract, Respondent's Exhibit 4, provides for that language in paragraph III(F), however, paragraph III(O)(B) Material Breach of Contract After Confirmation of Pregnancy, states that if the Surrogate is the breaching party and if after the birth of the child, the child is not healthy and/or is abnormal as a result of the Surrogate's breach, then all compensation and reimbursement shall be forfeited by the Surrogate. This contradicts subparagraph (g) of the statute and paragraph III(F) of the contract. This provision also appears to be in contravention of 63.213(3)(a), Fla. Stat. which provides that a Pre-Plan Adoption Agreement shall not contain any provision to "reduce any amount paid to the volunteer mother if the child....is born alive but impaired".

D. As a result of the foregoing observations, the Court has serious concern as to whether or not there was an executed contract, a meeting of the minds or a contract that complies with that Statute. Additionally, 742.14,Fla. Stat., provides that the donor of any ....sperm...., other than....a father who has executed a Pre-Planned Adoption Agreement under 63.212, Fla. Stat., shall relinquish all maternal or paternal rights and obligations with respect to the donation of the resulting children. In the case of Lamaritata v. Lucas, 823 So. 2d 316 (Fla. 2nd DCA, 2002), the Court made it clear that a donor who was not a commissioning couple or a father who has executed a Pre-Adoption Agreement had no parental rights. As such the Court believes that it is inappropriate to establish custody or provide for visitation between the child and the Respondent until these issues have been determined by the Court.

It is, therefore

ORDERED AND ADJUDGED:

The Respondent's Second Emergency Motion for Custody and Visitation be and the same is hereby DENIED until such time as the Court makes a ruling on the threshold issue of whether or not the Respondent's Exhibit 4 is a duly executed and binding Pre-Planned Adoption Agreement as required by and in compliance with 63.213, Fla. Stat. which was not revoked by the parties at any time prior to birth of the child. The Court believes that the parties should be allowed to present whatever additional evidence, if any, they may have with regard to these threshold issues and will schedule a hearing there on upon request of either party.

DONE AND ORDERED in Chambers at Jacksonville, Duval County, Florida, this 3 day of August, 2007.

The judge's decision denying us temporary custody was a big blow to us. But Tom still felt positive that this was all going to turn out for the best.

I couldn't shake the feeling that this judge had already made up his mind before we ever went to this first hearing. I felt deep down that this judge had no intention of giving us this baby. If he was planning on giving us the child, he would have given us temporary custody.

As we prepared for the trial our attorney promised to depose some witnesses that we had – or so he told us.

Our attorney had asked us to give him names, addresses, and phone numbers of people who we thought would be crucial to our case. But the judge had told the attorneys for both sides that there would be no he-said/she-said testimony. So some of the witnesses we had on our list we now would not be able to use the day of our trial. We wondered how it was possible that the judge didn't want to know what kind of person this surrogate was, and if she was capable of taking care of this child or even her own children, for that matter.

We thought this didn't sound like a court that was prepared to make a decision regarding what was in the best interests of the child. But we thought if we could prove that we were scammed, and that there was fraud, that would be all we needed.

Jennifer had already admitted in the first hearing that there was a contract, and had told the court that she took the first payment for the surrogacy, which our attorney said ratified the contract. And she admitted in the hearing that she was trying to get more money out of us by telling us she was going to give birth to the baby in the hospital when in reality she ended up birthing the baby at home. So even though we were disappointed about the judge's decision not to give us at the least visitation, we were still hopeful we could win.

Later we would obtain the transcript of the hearing from the court reporter, and then we could pull out discrepancies in Jennifer's story. We can tell you there were many discrepancies and contradictions in her story. How much more did this judge need to believe that she was trying to defraud us? We thought at least he would have to agree that Jennifer was trying to get more money out of us. It seemed like the next six weeks between the hearing and the trial would take forever.

We gave our attorney all the information he had requested, but as time went along it didn't seem to us that he was going after the people we thought were crucial to testify or that needed to be deposed, especially the witnesses to prove our point of fraud in this case. In the meantime, our attorney contacted us via e-mail that he had received the transcript from the hearing on July 31, 2007.

Here is some of the testimony during that hearing from page 42 of the transcript (our attorney questioning Jennifer):

The Court: Let him finish the question.

Surrogate: I'm sorry.

The Court: That's all right. That might have been all he was asking you but I don't know for sure that he was revoking - what he meant revoking of.

Our Attorney:

Q: Did you ever inform Mr. Lamitina that you were revoking the – for lack of a better term, the custody of the child and that you were going to retain the child?

A: Yes, sir.

Q: And that would be by virtue of the contract that you had drafted?

A: I'm sorry, I don't understand.

Q: Well, you had drafted a contract for him to sign –

A: Yes sir.

Q: – Correct? Okay. And in that contract there was a term where it stated that you had a certain amount of time pursuant to Florida law to revoke, correct?

A: I don't know if I was doing it as per the contract or just in a general I understand you're the father I'm – I want the baby.

Q: Okay. But that was also listed in the agreement?

A: I believe it was.

Q: Okay. And so then, therefore, you would have issued the revocation based not only the contract but also based on Florida law?

Attorney for Surrogate: Objection, Your Honor, relevancy.

Our Attorney: You can't look at your lawyer.

The Court: Sustained.

Surrogate: I don't understand what you are asking anyhow.

The Court: That's all right. I sustained the objection. Ask a different question.

Our Attorney:

Q: When did you inform him of the revocation?

A: I believe it was January or February through [attorney for surrogate].

Q: So it's your position that [your attorney] issued a letter to Mr. Lamitina that stated that you were officially revoking?

A: I don't know if it's technically those terms but yes.

Q: Isn't it true that there were letters sent back and forth where there were allegations that there was no contract?

A: Oh, yes.

Q: But there was nothing ever stated that you were revoking the contract; is that correct?

A: I don't know. I couldn't say for 100 percent accuracy.

Q: Okay. So when I asked you before, you really weren't sure?

A: Well, I don't – I said I did not know if that was part of the contract or not.

Q: Okay. Now, Mr. Lamitina presented you with a letter which purportedly held you in breach, correct?

A: Yes, he did.

Q: Okay. And you then sent him the response which we had admitted into evidence as Respondent's 1.

Our Attorney: Your Honor, may I show it to her?

Our Attorney:

Q: Do you recognize that e-mail?

A: Yes, I do.

Q: Okay. Is that an e-mail that you had sent to Mr. Lamitina?

A: Yes, sir.

Q: And what was the date on that?

A: ...If you agree, it's 24 of October.

Q: Okay. Now, in the response, you refer to language in the agreement–

A: Yes, sir.

Q: –correct?

A: Yes, sir

Q: Okay. And it was your position at the time that you were going to use the language in the contract–

A: Yes, sir.

Q: –for you to seek additional monies per home birth?

A: Yes.

Q: Correct?

A: Yes, sir.

Q: Okay. So in order for you to have done that you must have then relied on the fact that there was in fact a contract?

A: At that point, I don't know to say yes or no to that answer. But at that point, I was still trying to – I knew that I had not signed the contract and I was still try-ing to save this as being a surrogacy.

Q: So – but you know that, as a surrogacy from your own experience, there has to be some form of agreement in place correct?

A: Yes.

Q: Okay. So by you saying that you wanted to save the surrogacy coupled with this response wouldn't it be reasonable then to believe that you acknowledged that there was a contract as a result of this writing?

A: I acknowledge that there was a contract.

Attorney for Surrogate: Objection, Your Honor It's a leading.

Our Attorney:

Q: Okay. So you acknowledge that there was a contract?

The Court: Hold on, Basis of the objection?

Attorney for Surrogate: Leading.

The Court: Sustained.

Our Attorney:

Q: Is it your understanding based on your prior testimony that you acknowledge this as a contract?

A: Yes.

Q: Now –

The Court: It seems like that's the same question

Our Attorney: I wasn't leading her

The Court: Oh, it wasn't? Okay. I think it was.

In this testimony, Jennifer admitted to the existence of a contract. And she also admitted that she was trying to get more money out of us by saying that she was going to birth the baby in a hospital when instead she had the baby at home. In the surrogacy contract she had written in a clause that if she birthed the baby in a hospital as opposed to birthing the baby at home she got more money.

In another part of the transcript of this same hearing, Jennifer claimed that she decided to keep the child on November 23, 2006; here is that portion of that transcript starting with page 59.

Attorney for Surrogate:

Q: How did Mr. Lamitina contact you?

A: On the yahoo.com.

Q: Okay. And did he send an e-mail stating that he did not want the baby?

A: Yes, and I did read it that way.

Attorney for Surrogate:

Q: At the time, you were contacted by Mr. Lamitina did you have any intent to, in fact, to have the baby and then them adopt it?

A: Yes.

Q: Okay. But that changed with Mr. Lamitina questioning whether he was the father?

Our Attorney: Objection, leading.

Attorney for Surrogate:

Q: Why did that change?

A: Okay. It changed the day he sent me that e-mail. I cannot give my daughter to someone that doesn't – to her father who doesn't want her.

Now if the surrogate decided to keep the child November 23, as she claimed in her testimony above – which is when Tom sent the e-mail saying he did not want the child – why were we sent a letter from her attorney on December 7, 2006, stating that they wanted to negotiate a contract to control the situation?

Why would you need a contract in December to determine whether or not we would get the child if Jennifer had decided in November 23 to keep the child? That is what made us think that Jennifer was trying to get her surrogacy fee on top of keeping the child and getting child support along with health and life insurance.

Jennifer also claimed that we were unfit parents. When questioned in this hearing about that, this was her response (page 50 of the transcript):

Our Attorney:

Q: It's your opinion that they [meaning Tom and I] would be able to provide a loving home, correct?

A: No.

Q: Okay. Even his wife?

A: No that's – correct. That is correct.

Q: Okay. And on what basis do you make that statement

A: The media. I have been divorced sir, and my ex-husband and I have a wonderful relationship in which we put our children first and Mr. Lamitina is not, by my observation, putting his child first when he's saying, whatever kind of negative things, allowing people to–based on his media's attention, say horrendous things about me on the Internet and putting his child in danger.

Q: And these horrible things on the Internet, you know that they are all his postings?

A: They are not his but he –

Q: So you can't prove –

The Court: Sir, counsel –

Our Attorney: Yes, Judge, I'm sorry.

The Court: That's the second time. Wait until she finishes her answer–

The Surrogate: If it weren't–

The Court: –just as I want to make sure she lets you finish your question.

Our Attorney: I apologize, Your Honor.

The Surrogate: If it weren't for him going to the media pretty much no one would know about this case, those threats would not have been made to me and my children, all of them.

Our Attorney: Well–so you can't attribute these online bloggers for lack of a better term, you can't attribute those quotes directly to him, you don't know that he made them?

A: He didn't type them but he caused them.

Q: Okay. So if – if someone had – strike that. You and your husband have this wonderful relationship?

A: Ex-husband, yes.

Q: Ex-husband, okay is he proud of the fact that you had a child with another man and you are not giving the man that right to see him?

Attorney for Surrogate: Objection Your Honor.

Surrogate: I'm not him.

Our Attorney: Okay.

The Court: I will sustain the objection.

Our Attorney: Did you make any attempts yourself, not your lawyers to contact Mr. [my husband's name] prior to him going to the media?

A: No, I was advised not to.

Q: Okay. And Mr. Lamitina going to the media the sole or material basis for your belief that he is not a fit and proper parent?

A: No, I have others.

As you can see by Jennifer's testimony, her evidence for us not being good parents was the fact that we went to the media. She said there were other reasons, but why weren't these reasons brought up when her attorney questioned her? We went to the media so that we could inform other people so this same tragedy wouldn't happen to them. And we hoped to find other people who had information related to this surrogate that might help us. Every time we went to the media and an interview was shown on our case, people came forward with information about Jennifer, even bloggers who reported things like Jennifer smoking throughout her pregnancy.

Someone even said that they knew Jennifer and claimed that her roommate Sue, for whom Jennifer supposedly did a gestational surrogacy, requiring eggs from the mother, had a hysterectomy and was not capable of having children. It was very hard to find out who these bloggers were, and how they knew Jennifer, but we could tell these were people who knew things that nobody else should have known about Jennifer, and what was going on in the case.

Here are the closing arguments from the hearing (beginning on page 63 of the transcript):

The Court: Let me hear your argument on both the issue of both the contract and the visitation custody situation.

Our Attorney: Your Honor, before I get to that, I would like to bring up one matter to the Court that Ms. [surrogate's name] is stating that in her opinion there was an agreement; however, she revoked through Mr. [attorney for surrogate] office, Mr. [attorney for surrogate], being co-counsel in this case, I'm obviously going to need to issue a subpoena to him and ask him as to what it is that he did. So my question would be: How would the court like me to proceed on that because I would like to know now if there was a revocation that he prepared and if so where is it.

The Court: Well, I don't know if he's – they haven't offered anything into evidence at this point to that effect and, you know, I guess you just play it out and see what happens.

Our Attorney: Okay, Your Honor – thanks, Judge. Your Honor, it is our position – may it please the court, it is our position that this petitioner knew what she what was getting into, she knew she was entering into an agreement with Mr. Lamitina for him to be the IP, the intended parent and for his wife Gwyn to be the adoptive mother. The contract was prepared by her. She admitted under oath that there was a contract. She admitted that in her e-mail, in response to the breach allegations, that she referenced that contract. She was also seeking monetary damages pursuant to that contract. And she states that she placed the advertisement voluntarily. She drafted the advertisement and she knew the language that was in there. She also stated that she met my clients, visited with them and at some point in time liked him. It seems as though all of the turn for the worst or the relationship soured when my client called her to ask about certain medical issues concerning the safety of the child.

Attorney for Surrogate: Objection, Your Honor, none of that was evidence.

The Court: It's argument.

Our Attorney: My client is the father of this child. There is no doubt about that. He is the father. She admits it. The pleadings stipulate to that and there is DNA test with respect to that.

The Court: All right. Well, let's –

Our Attorney: So, the only question then would be for temporary custody and visitation. It would be our position that he is the father. He should be entitled to liberal and reasonable visitation, at a bare minimum; however, he should be entitled to temporary custody due to the fact that was the intent of the parties and the legislative intent. In many states, aside from Florida, they look behind – beyond the contract and behind the statute and they raise the bar on the best interest standard. It's not just what's in the best interest but it's what was the manifested intent of the parties. The intent of the parties, clearly by virtue of her accepting payment, engaging in e-mails, having artificial insemination was for my client to be the father and to take this child as his own and have his wife as the adoptive mother. It wasn't until at some point there was a change of heart on her part; however, there has been no evidence presented as to any element of revocation. She stated that she revoked but nothing is in evidence. Then she stated that her lawyer revoked, there is nothing in evidence. And she admitted that there was an agreement. So, as a result of that, Your Honor, my client should be given temporary custody pending a final hearing. The fact that the child is breastfeeding, the child shouldn't be breastfeeding because the child should be with my client. The fact that the child is two and a half months old, my client has the present ability to be loving and caring and nurturing father. They prepared for this. They have the necessary equipment and we would ask, Your Honor, that temporary custody be placed with Mr. and Mrs. [our name] pending further order of the court and that we have this matter proceed to final hearing as quickly as possible.

The Court: Thank you, sir.

Attorney for Surrogate: This is a – what comes down to basically a custody matter, Your Honor. There have been a lot of red herrings thrown out there as to whether there was a contract, if there was a breach of contract or some sort of fraud imposed – done by Ms. [surrogate's name] onto Mr. [my husband's name], there's no doubt that she was inseminated by his sperm. We have DNA test; however, whether there was a contract – or whether there was a contract or not is not even important in this case. There is no statute that specifically addresses traditional surrogacy in this state other than the pre-planned adoption statute. Florida Statute 63.213 2007, which clearly in that statute and unambiguously, it says that the mother who is going to place her child for adoption can revoke and decide to keep that child up until–at any point up until 48 hours following the birth and, you know, unless the court comes in and makes some determination that she is unfit, whether there is contract or not, doesn't even matter. There could be a contract in place signed by both parties and she can still come back and decide that she wants to keep this child. Ms. [surrogate's name] has decided – and I will go ahead and give, Your Honor, and opposing counsel a copy of the statute – the pre-planned adoptive statute. Ms. [surrogate's name] decided, after the strange things that began happening, you know, her intent was to give Mr. [my husband's name] a child and that's why she was inseminated and then he started questioning whether he was the father even though she went to his house to be artificially inseminated and, you know, doing different things like not going to take the test and, finally, she said, "I don't believe this guy is the person I should give my child to." And I think that the court has to directly look at Florida Statute 61.13. 61.13 in which it says that the court has to look to the best interest of the child and determine who has custody and that – several factors including – including who would preserve a loving and nurturing relationship towards the other parent has to be figured into that. Ms. [surrogate's name] doesn't believe that Mr. Lamitina would provide that or that he would, in fact, provide a loving and caring environment. She is a school teacher. She teaches young kids. She, in fact, takes care of kids for a living and she is fully prepared and equipped to take care of and mother her child.

The Court: All right. Thank you. Anything in rebuttal?

Our Attorney: Yes, Your Honor. The traditional surrogacy is not recognized under Florida statute; however, there is some correlation to the pre-planned adoption statute. It is not a debate as to whether or not she can revoke. The question is did she revoke and if she did revoke, when did she do it. Based on the evidence and the testimony presented, there is no revocation. I didn't see any documents. There is nothing presented into evidence, there was no revocation. So, for them to rely on the statute, it's a sword and it's a shield. You can't rely on it on one hand but disavow it on the other hand. The intent as my opposing counsel even stated her intent was to give Mr. Lamitina a child, period end of story. There can no longer be any – well, if she didn't like this, she didn't like that, she didn't like this, that's all irrelevant. It's the intent of the parties. And as to the reasons why my client had doubt, that stuff didn't come out evidentiary. They could have cross-examined him on that but they didn't. The fact of the matter is what was the intent of the parties, what happened and did she revoke. The intent of the parties clearly was for my client to have the child. The intent of the parties was for her to withdraw her parental rights and under the law, if she wanted to revoke, she could have but she didn't. If she did, it would have been here. It would have been the pink elephant in the living room.

The Court: All right. I'm going to take it under advisement and review the evidence and I will give you a written ruling as soon as I can. I appreciate everybody's presentations today.

Our Attorney: Your Honor, while my clients are in town, can I ask that they exercise some parental visitation while they are here?

The Court: Let me make a ruling first, okay. If he's going to be the father and have parental rights, he has got a long way ahead of him and he can make up a day or two and I want to make sure I'm doing what is right before I start that, okay?

As I mentioned before – how could the judge state that my husband had "a long way ahead of him" if he was going to be a father and have parental

90

rights? Now if this didn't sound like the judge had made up his mind already I don't know what would. You make the call. What do you think? To me it is pretty clear what this judge was thinking already.

We knew that we needed to keep forging on to get whatever information we could on Jennifer and the clock was ticking. We felt that the midwife and OB/GYN should have crucial information that would be vital to our case, number one being the traditional surrogacy contract. We knew from doing our first surrogacy that the midwife was supposed to have the traditional surrogacy contract signed by all parties involved in the surrogacy.

When we spoke to the midwife previously over the phone, she had divulged that she had done a surrogacy with Jennifer before. We, along with our attorney, were thinking that this previous surrogacy the midwife had been involved with was possibly the third child living with Jennifer and her roommate.

And if this was true, maybe then we could find out if it had been a gestational surrogacy as Jennifer claimed. We were thinking more than likely this was a traditional surrogacy that had gone wrong – there were just too many discrepancies.

There was also a person of interest we wanted to talk to, the man who was named as a sperm donor in the alleged gestational surrogacy. We found out from the paperwork obtained through court records that this sperm donor for Jennifer and Sue lived in Delaware.

We wanted to find out if this man really was a sperm donor and what had transpired between him and Jennifer. But we were not sure that this sperm donor could or would tell us what we wanted to know. It seemed extremely unlikely to us that this man, who lived in Delaware, would have taken time off work to fly down to Ft. Myers, to sign papers that he was a sperm donor, then sign an affidavit that he would have no rights to the child in this alleged gestational surrogacy. Why was this done 13 months after the child was born, instead of three days as was required by law according to our attorney? Why would the sperm donor be signing his rights away at that point?

If it was the sperm donor's intention to not have any rights to the child from the beginning, the clinic Jennifer used would have, for the protection of the sperm donor, required the sperm donor to sign his rights away, thus keeping Jennifer from coming after him at a later date for child support.

It didn't make sense to us. No matter how much you think you know somebody, I won't trust someone's word over it being written on a contract. Not anymore. If we had learned anything, it was that you have to get everything in writing; even anticipated things that could happen should be in writing.

Let's face it, we live in society where you can get sued and taken to court for just about anything nowadays. Whether it is fact or fiction is anybody's guess.

# Chapter 7

# The Trial

The day of the trial arrived. We met with our attorney before the trial and were told that our attorney didn't bother to subpoena the midwife. Little did we know that almost a year later we would finally get the medical records from the midwife, but we would never get a chance to actually question her on the witness stand.

As mentioned, the midwife had told us previously in a phone conversation that Jennifer had done another surrogacy with her, and we were dying to know if this midwife knew if it had been a gestational surrogacy with clinic records or a traditional surrogacy, as we suspected.

We wanted to question the midwife on the details. Did the midwife get the paperwork from the clinic? If Jennifer had done a gestational surrogacy as she claimed, the midwife should have the paperwork. We suspected that this gestational surrogacy was in fact really a traditional surrogacy that had gone wrong, like ours.

But we needed evidence that we thought the midwife or OB/GYN should have. Why was our attorney not trying to get this information that he said we needed to prove fraud?

During the trial when Jennifer was testifying, she was asked why she didn't sign the contract. Her response was that she didn't sign it because it was obviously not important for us to sign the contract before she got pregnant, so she didn't sign it. But she had no problem cashing the check after we signed the contract.

Her answer to that was that no, she had no problem cashing our check at all. In fact, her answers to the questions from our attorney seemed arrogant, as if she was thinking, "What are you going to do about it?" We wondered why she even bothered to have us sign the contract at all

Jennifer was adamant that we get the contract signed and notarized before we left to go on our wedding vacation. Yet she was testifying under oath that she didn't sign the contract herself and blamed us as the reason why she didn't sign it. So why accept the first payment for the contract? We thought Jennifer had been leading us on, making us believe at this point everything was normal and that we still had a contract.

We thought a blind man could see what was going on. We wondered how long this illusion of having a contract and a surrogacy could have gone on. If we had not caught Jennifer smoking at our home and then discovered the genetic abnormality in her family that last weekend she came to our home, we would have continued to pay her until the entire surrogacy fee had been paid, along with the medical bills. We were thinking that Jennifer was planning to get her surrogacy fee in addition to child support because she did not sign the surrogacy contract. She obviously planned to keep the baby and get child support, health and life insurance with herself as the beneficiary. Not only that, but Jennifer wanted Tom to sign his rights away. As if we would actually agree to such terms.

As the trial continued, our attorney began to call witnesses to testify on our behalf. One of the witnesses called to testify for us was our first surrogate. Jennifer and her attorney were trying to say that we would not raise our daughter in a loving environment.

Our former surrogate was there to confirm that this was not true and that you only had to look at our son to see that he was very happy and well behaved, and that as our former surrogate she felt free to be a part of our son's life. She said she was able to have an ongoing relationship with us and our son as well, and that she felt like family. This was definitely not what the opposing attorney and Jennifer wanted the judge to hear.

Our attorney called another witness, a nice lady who, up until the day of the first hearing, we had never met. This woman said she felt compelled to come forward and speak on our behalf as to the kind of person Jennifer was, based on her experience. This woman went on the stand and testified that she had Jennifer watch her son while she worked.

At that time Jennifer was running a daycare out of her home. This woman testified that she brought her son to Jennifer to take care of him. This lasted only three days because each time, at the end of the day when she picked up her son, he was dirty and smelled like smoke.

The witness said Jennifer's house was always filthy. On one of the days that she dropped off her son, Jennifer suggested to her that she should do a surrogacy – she could make $30,000 a year, stay home and not have to work.

On the third and final day when this woman dropped off her son at Jennifer's house, she was running late and did not have time to change her son out of his pajamas. She asked Jennifer if she would mind dressing him with the clothing she had brought with her. Jennifer agreed.

The woman noticed when she dropped off her son that Jennifer was still in her pajamas as well, but at the time she did not think too much about it. At the end of the day, when she returned to pick up her son, she noticed not only had Jennifer not bothered to take off her son's pajamas and put on his regular clothes, but again he was very dirty and smelled like smoke.

Not only that, Jennifer had not bothered to get out of her own pajamas and was still wearing them at 5 p.m. When the witness arrived to pick up her son, Jennifer was holding the boy while puffing on a cigarette. It was at that time the woman told Jennifer that her son would not be returning.

As our witness was testifying about this situation, the judge kept trying to cut her off. At this point we felt like the judge had definitely made up his mind. He did not appear to have any interest in knowing whether this surrogate was stable psychologically and able to raise our daughter in the way that would be best for the child.

This judge was supposed to be looking out for the best interests of the child; it didn't seem to be going in that direction at all. The judge did not feel that Jennifer's behavior or the conditions in which this child was to be raised were of importance. The only thing he was concerned with was whether or not this was a legal contract.

He was not even concerned whether or not Jennifer was committing fraud. We'd also like to note that Jennifer had no witnesses to testify on her behalf. We thought that at least Sue – Jennifer's roommate/adoptive mother/associate/domestic partner, or whatever title Jennifer wanted to give her – would have testified on her behalf.

Several people in the courtroom appeared to us to be ready to testify on Jennifer's behalf. But we knew that her attorney had not listed any witnesses on the witness list. In fact, Jennifer had not one witness testify for her at the trial. We thought that was odd.

We would find out later that Jennifer would not need Sue, or anyone else for that matter, to testify. As the trial was winding down, the attorneys were to present their closing arguments to the judge. Our attorney was first to give his closing argument and as he did this we could not believe what we were seeing.

As our attorney was giving his closing argument for our case to the judge, the judge's behavior was shockingly unprofessional. The judge slumped down in his chair, lay his head back, and looked up to the ceiling. He even yawned at one point as if he was bored out of his mind, and appeared ready to fall asleep.

We could not believe what we were seeing. This was a civil court judge! We were amazed at the judge's lack of professionalism. The judge did not seem to be the least worried that this behavior was being broadcast on local and national news on live television.

Our attorney finished his argument and Jennifer's attorney got up to give his closing argument. The judge sat up straight in his seat, and looked directly at the opposing attorney, hanging on every word.

We thought it was just incredible that a judge would behave this way. The judge seemed a little disappointed that the attorney's only closing argument was that there was no contract because Jennifer never signed it. But if there was a contract, Jennifer revoked it. Jennifer's attorney went on to say that whether there was a contract or not, Jennifer was the biological mother of this child and had a right to keep this child if she so chose. Yet no revocation letter was ever entered into evidence by her attorney nor was any such letter ever sent to us or our attorney.

According to our attorney, under Florida statutes, with a contract of any kind, whether for a surrogacy or some other purpose, a revocation must be written and sent by certified mail with copies sent to the attorneys as well. At the end of closing statement, Jennifer's attorney tried to enter a letter which he claimed was a revocation, but our attorney objected since there was no evidence before that day that this letter of revocation ever existed.

Our attorney argued that this alleged revocation letter was a fraud and that if this letter had existed before that day, Jennifer's attorney would have produced it earlier and we would not even be having this trial. But if this revocation letter was sent to us, as Jennifer's attorney claimed, why not testify to the validity of the letter?

We ascertained that it could possibly be a strategy by Jennifer's attorney; or maybe the opposing counsel was trying to pull a fast one. Whatever it was, it didn't work. They were not allowed to enter it into evidence.

Besides that, why try to enter a revocation letter into evidence if it would only be needed if there was a contract? And since they were arguing that there was no contract, why would Jennifer's attorneys even try to enter the letter into evidence in the first place? We thought that we knew why, but we couldn't prove it.

So after the trial proceedings were over, the press was waiting outside the courtroom, including a reporter from the television show *Inside Edition* who wanted to do an interview with us.

We were surprised since this was a show that only did exclusives; other local and national media had reported our story previously. So we talked with local and national media and answered the questions that we could. We scheduled an interview for later that day with *Inside Edition* to be held at the hotel where our attorney was staying.

After the interviews at the courthouse were over, we spoke to our attorney to see what he thought of the trial. We wanted to know if he felt the same way we did about the judge and his behavior when our attorney was giving his closing argument. But our attorney had a whole different perspective; he thought the judge was concentrating. Concentrating on what?! We thought the judge looked like he was about to commit hara-kiri at any time.

We told our attorney what we thought, but he tried to make us believe we were wrong. Our attorney thought we were going to win this case, but we just couldn't get out of our heads the way the judge reacted and his behavior during the trial. We were definitely not as positive and we kept wondering why the fraud was not brought up in this case during the trial.

When we asked our attorney why the fraud was not being addressed, he kept saying that this was family court and that the fraud would be a different case we would need to address in civil or criminal court. We would find out that was not true, but it was too late in this trial to bring up the fraud.

When we got back to our attorney's hotel, the *Inside Edition* reporter and her camera men were setting up for the interview with us and our attorney. When everything was ready we sat down to be interviewed. The first question the reporter asked was how we thought the trial went that day. We responded that we were not sure, but we had Jennifer's testimony – she acknowledged the contract, she took the proceeds from the contract making the contract binding, and there was no legal evidence of a written revocation.

So our attorney pointed out whether it was legal as a surrogacy contract or not, it was still a binding contract. He also mentioned to the reporter that the alleged revocation letter was not sent certified mail as it should have been by Jennifer's counsel, but was alleged to have been sent by regular mail.

Jennifer's attorney claimed the alleged revocation letter was supposedly sent and dated the same date as a letter we did receive on January 18, 2007, which did not in any way state that Jennifer was revoking the contract, but only stated that this was going to become a child support issue. Why would Jennifer's attorney have to send two letters the same day, both letters nearly identical except for some different wording on the alleged revocation letter?

But even if this revocation letter had been sent as alleged, no letter dated January 18 specifically stated a revocation of the contract as law required, according to our attorney as well as other attorneys watching this case. And if this alleged revocation existed all along, this case would have been over a long time ago. Why would you need to revoke a contract that you never signed?

It was as if Jennifer's attorney was playing both sides of this lawsuit. Just in case the judge ruled that this surrogacy contract was binding, he wanted to make sure they had both issues covered, especially since Jennifer took the proceeds from the contract. It didn't look good as contract law goes.

The *Inside Edition* interview was quite long and when we were done we asked the reporter when it would air. The reporter told us it should be within the week. We kept looking for the interview but never saw it. We thought maybe we missed it or that they just decided not to air it.

So we called *Inside Edition* to verify with the reporter if our interview had been aired or not, but *Inside Edition* told us no – it would probably air within the next few days. It never did. We would find out almost eight months later that the story was not aired by *Inside Edition* because they were trying to talk Jennifer into giving her side of the story – that way it would be an exclusive for the show.

Jennifer finally did agree to speak to *Inside Edition* and give her story. It was aired in May of 2008. The *Inside Edition* reporter gave us a call the day before and told us they were finally airing our story, failing to mention they had also interviewed Jennifer. That was surprising to us, but our intuition had been correct that the show would try to get Jennifer's side of the story.

When this interview aired, we saw our daughter for the first time. She was so cute. She had Tom's blue eyes and curly hair.

It was sad and hard to watch this little girl – a little girl who we thought would have been home with us. We had wondered if the little girl would look like Tom, as our son from the first surrogacy did. But she did not look as much like Tom – we could only see a resemblance.

As we looked at the pictures, we thought that our daughter looked sad. We didn't know if we were just imagining she looked sad or if we were somehow secretly wishing in some way, even though she had never met us, that our daughter could sense that there was something not right or that someone was missing in her life. But how could she? She didn't even know that we existed, that there was a father and a mother out there who loved her very much.

But when other friends and family saw our daughter on *Inside Edition*, they got the same impression of sadness – there was a look about her, they said.

We thought the same thing but we had not mentioned to anyone how we felt about the interview. Our friends went on to say that they could tell the reporter for *Inside Edition* was trying to get our daughter to smile or laugh, but she never gave the reporters that big beautiful smile they have so often seen on our son.

Our son smiles all the time and would smile at anyone. His smile lights up a room. He is such a blessing to us.

The day after the trial, our attorney told us that he sent an e-mail to Jennifer's attorney, questioning the method in which he tried to enter the alleged revocation into evidence during the trial.

This is the e-mail that our attorney sent to Jennifer's attorney:

[surrogate's attorney]:

After we left the hearing yesterday I had thoughts and concerns over the letter that [co-counsel] allegedly sent on Jan 18. I would like to discuss it with you. I have concerns over why it was not attempted to be entered in to evidence through [co-counsel]. You tried to get it in through every other witness, but not through the author who was in the courtroom.

It is making me question the authenticity of the letter and why [co-counsel] didn't testify that he wrote it. If this is lawyer's strategy, that is one thing, but I am having concerns of whether that letter was actually mailed.

Please let me know and settle my assurances that the letter was not a fraud and was attempted to be entered in to evidence through everyone but the author, and why you made reference to it in your closing when it was never admitted into evidence.

This is a matter of great concern and very important as I need to know these answers to satisfy my ethical responsibilities to the court and to the Florida Bar. I am sure that you can appreciate my position and why I need these concerns set aside.

Jennifer's attorney then faxed our attorney the alleged revocation letter that Jennifer's attorney says that he sent us on January 18, a letter that we miraculously never received:

Dear Mr. Lamitina:

This letter is to memorialize our final conversation. As we discussed, [the surrogate] has decided to keep the child. As such, this is now a family law issue. This firm has withdrawn from representation of [the surrogate] and all future correspondence should be directed to her new counsel [name of new attorney and his contact information].

After our attorney received this fax, he asked Jennifer's attorney how this letter was sent because we never received it. That's when Jennifer's attorney claimed the alleged revocation letter was sent by regular mail.

Our attorney was very suspicious and even went so far as to contact our prior counsel just to make sure that this letter had never been received or maybe misplaced and not included in the paperwork that our present counsel had received. However, all important paperwork received by our prior counsel had been transferred over to our present counsel.

This revocation letter was never sent to our prior attorney or to us. This letter was dated the same date as the January 18 letter stating this had become a child support issue. Nowhere did the letter we received or the alleged revocation letter state they were revoking the contract.

Our attorney told us that according to Florida law Jennifer would have had to state specifically that she was revoking the contract in the letter sent to us by her attorney. The necessary wording was not there.

A revocation letter for this surrogacy would have had to be sent certified mail so that Jennifer's attorney would have proof that the revocation letter was sent by him, and received and signed for by us, showing proof we had received it. We never signed for it because it was never sent.

This, in our opinion and that of our attorney, was an attempted fraud by Jennifer's attorneys because they were trying to cover both sides of the law.

It seemed suspicious to us that we and our prior counsel received only the one letter on January 18, but not this other letter they allegedly sent out the same day, stating that Jennifer decided to keep the child. Jennifer's attorney never entered this revocation letter into evidence.

Why? We believe that the surrogate's attorneys knew they would be in big trouble had they tried to testify to the validity of that alleged revocation letter. So was this a strategy by Jennifer's attorney, or something else? Jennifer's attorney sending this alleged revocation letter to our attorney by fax would lead you to believe this could be federal fraud, because he would not validate the letter by testifying to its validity under oath in court.

Our attorney said the letter was never sent certified mail, and only showed up as a revocation sent to our attorney over the fax.

Would these attorneys actually put their licenses on the line for this case and this person? We definitely knew there was something underhanded going on and neither we nor our attorney liked it.

# Chapter 8

# The Final Verdict

$A$fter waiting what seemed like forever to receive word from the judge, we finally got a verdict. A whole month had passed and we were hoping and praying that this nightmare would soon be over and our daughter would finally be coming home to us. The reporters had been calling us off and on during this period, trying to find out if a verdict had been rendered by the judge.

The reporters were sure we would be getting custody of our daughter and they wanted to be there when we picked her up and then follow us home. When the judge had reached a verdict, he sent it over to our attorney. Then our attorney e-mailed it to us.

Our attorney gave us a brief overview of what we would be reading and we were devastated. After all this, we would not be bringing our daughter home. How could it be, that after all the evidence and testimony presented to the judge, he could render such a verdict? We may never know.

This is the verdict that was rendered by the judge:

## FINAL JUDGMENT ON PETITION TO DETERMINE PATERNITY AND COUNTER-PETITION

The cause came before the court for hearing again on September 12, 2007 for the court to receive additional testimony and evidence concerning whether or not the parties had a valid and binding Contract or whether or not the Petitioner rescinded the Contract. This Court previously conducted a hearing on August 1, 2007 and entered an Order August 3, 2007, based upon that testimony and evidence. Upon all the evidence, the Court makes the following additional findings of fact.

A. The Traditional Surrogacy Contract "Pre-Adoption Plan", Respondent's Exhibit #4, was in fact prepared by the Petitioner; however the document was prepared by her at the request of the Respondent, Mr. Lamitina, on the representation that this was the same Contract he had used in his previous surrogacy and that it was a Contract which was also available online at www.surromomsonline.com. As such, he requested that she merely draft the same document that he had used before and insert the correct names.

B. The Petitioner became pregnant on or about August 21, 2006, and the Respondent signed the document on or about September 6, 2006. After the Petitioner received the Respondent's e-mail of November 23, 2006, Petitioner's Exhibit #2, wherein he indicated he did not want the baby, she decided then that she wanted to revoke the Contract. Petitioner hired [surrogate's attorney], Esquire to be her attorney and believed that [surrogate's attorney], Esquire wrote a letter to Respondent advising him that she was revoking the Contract. Petitioner stated that she also believed that [surrogate's attorney] had talked to Respondent on the phone several times and told Respondent that she was revoking the Contract. One of the reasons she believes that the Respondent knew she was revoking the Contract is that his prior surrogate mother put an e-mail on the www.surromomsonline.com website proclaiming the Petitioner was revoking the Agreement, Petitioner's Exhibit #3. On February 7, 2007, Petitioner saw this e-mail and the only way that the former surrogate, [our prior surrogate's name], would have know Petitioner had revoked the Contract would have been by the Respondent telling her.

C. On September 25, 2006, Petitioner received a check for $1500.00 from the Respondent which she cashed.

D. Mr. Lamitina testified that he did not intend to revoke the Contract when he said he did not want the baby. He was trying to get a response from the Petitioner because at the time she was not communicating with him. He admitted that on one occasion he told [surrogate's attorney] that he did not want the child and asked [surrogate's attorney] to send him an Affidavit of Non-Paternity. He claims he was under stress because of [surrogate's attorney] pushing him to schedule the DNA test when it was not convenient for his schedule. When he got the Affidavit of Non-Paternity he did not sign it.

E. Respondent received a letter from [surrogate's attorney] on December 14, 2006, Petitioner's Exhibit #4, and on January 15, 2007, [surrogate's attorney] told him that Petitioner was revoking the Contract. That same date, Respondent told [our prior surrogate] by e-mail that Petitioner was revoking the Contract.

F. Respondent did not execute any preplanned adoption agreement which complied with the requirements of section 63.213, Florida Statutes (2006). Respondent did, however donate sperm for the purpose of inseminating Petitioner.

G. The child in this case was conceived by artificial insemination at the home of Petitioner or the home of Respondent. No evidence of laboratory handling of human eggs or pre-embryos was introduced; therefore, "assisted reproductive technology," as defined in section 742.13(1), Florida Statutes (2006), was not involved in this case. Because assisted reproductive technology was not used, Respondent and his wife were not a "commissioning couple" as defined in section 742.13(2), Florida Statutes (2006).

## Conclusions of Law

H. In Lamaritata V. Lucas, 823 So. 2d 316 (Fla. 2d DCA 2002), the parties agreement provided for donation of sperm and, "if childbirth resulted, the donor would have no parental rights and obligations associated with the delivery, and both parties would be foreclosed from establishing those rights and obligations by the institution of an action to determine paternity of any such child or children." Lamaritata 823 So. 2d at 318. The court's reversal of the trial court's award of visitation to the donor was based alternatively on the agreement of the parties and on section 742.14, Florida Statutes; the court opined that if the statute were applicable, "the donor, whether or not he is scientifically determined to be the biological parent..., will be foreclosed from all parental rights, including his access to the children. Id. (quoting and adding emphasis to. L.A.L. v. D.A.L.

Section 742.14, Florida Statutes (2006) provides, in relevant part, "The donor of any egg, sperm, or pre-embryo, other than the commissioning couple or a father who has executed a preplanned adoption agreement under s. 63.212, shall relinquish all maternal or paternal rights and obligations with respect to the donation or the resulting children." 714 So. 2d 595, 596 (Fla. 2d DCA 1998). Recognizing that "sperm donor" is not defined in the statute, the Lamaritata court found the term applicable based on the parties' agreement. Id. Though factually distinguishable, the Court finds Lamaritata persuasive for its reliance on section 742.14, Florida Statutes to determine that a sperm donor who has not executed a preplanned adoption agreement which complies with section 63.212 (now section 63.213, see Ch. 2003-58 §§ 35-36, at 62-68, Laws of Fla.) has no parental rights or obligations. Though Respondent, unlike the donor in Lamaritata, did not execute an agreement stating his intent to relinquish parental rights and obligations, the Court concludes that Respondent did relinquish parental rights and obligations by operation of law.

I.  The parties met over the internet. This preamble has become an all-too-commonplace event in our society. It is clear that the internet has been positive development in our society. It has opened our lives to many improved and advanced abilities; however, there are drawbacks. In the Court's opinion, this is an example of one of them. The Respondent did not engage the services of an attorney who could have insured that his rights and obligations were protected. Instead he relied upon a document he had used before which he apparently got off the internet. In addition, he did not have a signed Contract upon which he could rely and enforce his rights to enable him to become a parent as he wished. The services of an experienced attorney who was familiar with the Florida Statute on Pre-Planned Adoption Agreement and contract law may have adequately protected him. In this case there is no Pre-Planned Adoption Agreement and contract that complies with section 63.213, Florida Statutes. The Court believes that the legislature has wisely considered the need for such an agreement in this type of situation. The emotional risks are too high not to have a binding written contract between the parties. The legislature has specifically stated what must be in such a Contract, at a minimum, and also provided important provisions that may not be contained in any written Pre-Planned Adoption Agreement. The Court's only conclusion is that the legislature intended for this to be the means and way by which surrogacy could be carried out. It is the Court's finding that there was never a Contract and that if there was one, the Petitioner/Mother terminated it.

It is, therefore

**ORDERED AND ADJUDGED:**

The Petitioner shall assume all parental rights and responsibilities for the child, [the child's name], as otherwise provided by law for a Mother and the Court does not approve the Pre-Planned Adoption pursuant to the Florida Adoption Act.

The Respondent has neither parental rights nor obligations with respect to the child, [the child's name].

**DONE AND ORDERED** in Chambers at Jacksonville, Duval County, Florida, this 10th day of October, 2007.

# Chapter 9

# The Appeal
# and the Fraud Case

$A$fter the crushing news that we had lost yet again, we consulted our attorney. We felt that this was the end. What else could we do? We were now out of money, and Tom's work had come to a standstill as the economy was collapsing.

After discussing with our attorney the situation with our finances and our discouragement with losing the second time, our attorney told us that he thought we should continue fighting for our daughter. We thought that was easy for him to say. We were not sure how or even if we would be able to go on with this case even if we wanted to – we could not pay our attorney any more money.

Not to mention the toll of riding the emotional roller coaster we were on. Our attorney was trying to convince us that a grave injustice had happened to us. This judge took away my husband's civil rights given to him by the Florida Supreme Court, that the right to parent a child without intrusion is a constitutional right. He said we had good grounds for an appeal and that if we would let him continue with this case, he would do it pro bono.

At this point we had lost our confidence in our attorney and the justice system. We kept asking our attorney why he didn't subpoena the midwife to testify. Why weren't a lot of things this attorney promised to do in this case done?

This attorney gave us the runaround, making excuses, telling us we could not bring charges of fraud against Jennifer in family court. We found out later from another attorney that this was not family court – it was civil court. We decided that if we were going to continue with this case, even if we had to pay for it and get the forms and fill them out ourselves, we were going to file charges of fraud against this woman.

So we agreed that we would appeal, but only if our attorney would file the fraud papers or at least prepare them, and we would do the rest. The fraud papers had to be served by the process server at Jennifer's workplace. It was at that time that we found out that Jennifer had resigned from her job as a teacher and was no longer working at the school. We sure wanted to know why Jennifer had resigned. She told us herself that she had signed a three-year contract to work for the school. We would find out much later why she had.

In the meantime, our attorney still continued to give us a hard time about how we wanted to proceed with this case. We wanted to add Sue to the fraud charge because she knew what was going on and was a part of the cover up of information about Jennifer – she had gone along with Jennifer's plan of deception.

During this period of time that we had retained this attorney to handle our case, we had obtained some information from bloggers about some legal problems he had.

At first we did not think much about the information. After all, if our attorney had committed such things as were being alleged by these bloggers, how could it be he was still practicing? But we did begin to wonder what was going on with him. We contacted him on numerous occasions to get updates on our case without getting any response, and we saw that he was moving his offices yet again.

Our attorney had just moved from his last location months earlier. When we would try to contact his office, the phone would be no longer in service. When we questioned the attorney's office staff, they would give us the excuse that the attorney was experiencing growth and had to move to accommodate it.

The trial was in September, the judge ruled on the case in October, and the appeal was finally submitted by our attorney sometime in December or January. Why was this taking so long just to file the paperwork for the appeal? Then, after our attorney filed the appeal, it seemed as if the appeal was just sitting there without any progress.

When we tried to get information out of our attorney, he tried to tell us that he was working on it, that it was a process of going back and forth between us and our attorney and Jennifer and her attorney. In the meantime, the fraud case was also sitting there without anything happening on it. After we asked our attorney if he was doing anything on our case, he sent us an e-mail saying that he lost our phone number. He said he was going to update us on the appeal and bring federal action and we could include the judge for violating Tom's rights.

But before we got this e-mail from our attorney we had received an e-mail from the three case workers who were supposed to be working on our case, saying that they had all resigned from working with our attorney. They would no longer be working our case.

This e-mail was sent not only to us, but to all of our attorney's clients. We began to wonder if the allegations we were hearing about this attorney were true. Then, in April, we found out from a blogger on the Internet that our appeal had been dropped.

In disbelief, we decided to contact the courthouse ourselves since we couldn't get any information directly from our attorney or his staff. When we called the courthouse, the clerk of the court told us that the appeal had been dropped on February 22.

When we asked the clerk of the court what happened, she said our attorney never filed the proper paperwork. As a result of his incompetence our appeal had been dropped. We asked the clerk of the court if this could be a mistake – we just couldn't wrap our minds around this when just a week before our attorney led us to believe that everything was going as planned.

We started getting e-mails from some other clients of our attorney. These clients alleged that our attorney had taken money from them and never done anything on their cases. It seemed he had scammed a lot of people out of money. He had not even filed any paperwork on most of these clients' cases. Before we knew it, the Federal Bureau of Investigation was involved, and our attorney was arrested. The Florida Bar Association was after him as well.

So here we were with no attorney, not knowing what we were going to do. How much more emotional stress could we take? It seemed as if it just wasn't meant for us to go on. How could we fight on when we had no money?

We called attorney after attorney and not one person was willing to take our case, especially if we were not going to be able to pay. So we thought this was it. We had found out through talking to some of these attorneys that once the appeal was dropped we could not appeal again. We were devastated. It seemed to us that door after door was closing.

Maybe it was time to give it up. We'd fought hard and long but we just could not go on. It was approaching a long two years of fighting for a child we had not even been allowed to see. The child was approaching her first birthday and we had missed so much of her life already.

In the meantime, Tom had to go in to get treatment at our chiropractor's office and he told the chiropractor our terrible story. The chiropractor told Tom that he thought he knew an attorney that would either take the case pro bono or at least work out a payment plan with us. He told us to give this attorney a call.

When my husband got home we discussed whether or not we should call this attorney. After all, attorneys were telling us that we were not going to be able to get our daughter. We had lost in the courts and we were tired and weary emotionally drained from our constant, two-year battle. We gave it some thought and decided it wouldn't hurt just to call and talk to this new attorney.

Around this time, we decided to go to a neighborhood event where local businesses and restaurants were giving out samples of food and information on different services in our area.

This was before the November election, and a lot of local officials were there campaigning. As we walked around checking things out, we happened to run into a man who was the father of the assistant district attorney of the county we lived in.

Tom began to tell him about our story and, after listening for a few minutes, he began to remember hearing about our case in the news. This man told us that his son was adopted, and had followed our case closely. It was a subject close to his heart, and both his son and he thought our case had been handled horribly. He said that his son would probably like to talk to us about the case and see if he could help us.

So the man took Tom's phone number and said he would have his son call us. When my husband heard this, he started to feel hope that maybe someone was finally seeing the fraud involving this surrogate. Hopefully now there was a chance, albeit a remote one, that we might still, be able to get our daughter.

We waited with anticipation for a couple of weeks and nothing happened; we never got a call from the assistant district attorney. It was at that time that we decided we were not ready to give up just yet. We knew in our hearts that if we stopped now, Jennifer could do this again to someone else. And from what we were hearing around the country, our case and what was happening to us was just the beginning.

Since our story came out in the media, we began to hear about other stories very similar to ours happening to other couples around the country. What was going on? Could this be a conspiracy being passed along somehow from woman to woman as a way to take advantage of unsuspecting parents desperate to have children?

The cases were so similar it was like they followed a script. Or was it something that had been going on all along, and our own experience just heightened our sensitivity to the cases similar to ours? We knew that we needed to expose it, bring it into the open, and make everyone who might get involved in a surrogacy aware of what can happen.

We had not received a call from the assistant district attorney, but my husband decided to take a chance and go down to the courthouse in person to pay him a visit, not knowing if he would even see Tom or not. When he entered the office and told the secretary that we had been referred by the assistant DA's father, the assistant DA came out into the waiting room to meet Tom.

He told Tom he was intrigued by our story and said that he was familiar with our case. But he thought that our case was a matter that should be taken up with the Feds and the Florida State Attorney General's Office. He said that we would have to prove the fraud in civil court first; after that, his office or the Florida State Attorney General's office could take it from there.

He thought that this surrogate had committed a felony because of the ad she had placed on the Internet and the use of letters and faxes that Jennifer and her attorneys had used made it a federal crime. Finally, someone else was on the same page as we were. Hearing this gave us a sense of hope, even if it was only a short reprieve. So we hired yet another attorney and the first thing he did was to subpoena the midwife's records.

This new attorney felt sure that if we subpoenaed Jennifer's midwife and OB/GYN, by law they should have a signed surrogacy contract. In Florida's surrogacy laws, you were supposed to have a surrogacy contract signed by both the surrogate and the intended parents before any medical care could be rendered to the surrogate.

Our attorney was confident that the midwife and OB/GYN would have a signed surrogacy contract because, if not, they risked a lawsuit themselves for not following protocol and the Florida statutes for surrogacies.

After waiting for months to get the records from the midwife, we found out that the midwife and OB/GYN did not get a signed surrogacy contract. Another letdown for us and our new attorney. And since the midwife had no proof of a surrogacy contract, we were now going to have to pursue a lawsuit against the midwife and OB/GYN for failing to follow the proper procedures for doing a surrogacy.

This new attorney felt that since this case was going to be more involved than he first thought, he decided that he didn't want to proceed any further as our attorney on this case. It seemed that no attorney was willing to put in the time necessary to winning this case. Most attorneys agreed our case was winnable, so what was the problem? We discussed where to go from here.

The assistant district attorney had indicated that this was a case for the Feds to handle and it was definitely fraud. So why couldn't we get these attorneys or someone to take this case and run with it? We decided that we would do some investigation of our own and gather as much information as we could find on Jennifer.

We started by trying to find out just exactly why Jennifer resigned from her place of employment. If she had signed a three-year contract with the school, the school would have not been happy that she decided to resign in the middle of her contract.

We called Jennifer's former school and asked if we could have copies of any and all of the school records relating to her. Tom also asked if we could have copies of any complaints made to the school about her. The school told us that not all the records were public, but that they would give us what they could and mail us the records. Tom asked if he could come to the school and pick up the paperwork himself.

We had a hunch there might be something surrounding Jennifer's resignation that might be of interest to us. Little did we know that we would get more than we bargained for.

At first glance at the paperwork, Tom did not think there was any information that we could use. But upon closer inspection, the school's papers showed why Jennifer had resigned from her job.

It was there in black and white. Could it be that even before she found out that our appeal was dropped Jennifer was pulling another scam? It was unbelievable. When we served the fraud papers back in January 2008, she had already resigned from the school. She had reported to the principal of the school that she had breast cancer and was going to have to undergo a radical mastectomy.

Investigation by the school ethics board showed that Jennifer had reported a bogus radical mastectomy and had faxed the school a forged doctor's letter from the Internet as an excuse for light duty upon returning to work. The conclusion of the school investigation was that the evidence against Jennifer was found to be sustained (to be true). She then gave her irrevocable resignation to the school.

The school's Office of Professional Standards began this investigation on January 15, 2008, and Jennifer was found to be in violation of the Florida Statute 1012.796. Now this was more evidence to show the court a pattern with this woman – she had done the same thing to the school that she had done to us. She used the Internet and faxed the school a forged letter from a doctor.

The findings were documented in a memo from the Professional Standards Office on February 5, 2008:

The Office of Professional Standards began an investigation on 01-15-08 involving [surrogate's name] who reported a bogus radical mastectomy to her Principal Ms. [principal's name] and provided a return to work Doctor's note requesting light duty. The Doctor's note was a forgery on letterhead which was generated from Dr. Scot Ackerman's web-site. The Doctor's note was not even a good facsimile.

[Surrogate's name] submitted an Irrevocable Letter of Resignation effective 02-06-08.

As a result of the investigation, the allegation is cleared as:

SUSTAINED: Evidence proves allegation(s) to be true.

What was Jennifer thinking? Did she think because she had gotten away with this scam in our case she could do it again? I mean, Jennifer did confess to doing exactly that in front of a judge and the judge did absolutely nothing about it. We decided to send this new information to the media to see what they thought, but only one local station was interested in reporting this new evidence we found. (During this time the Florida media was focused on the Caylee Anthony child murder investigation.)

This station was located in the town where Jennifer lived. When the reporter called Jennifer to get a comment, she told the reporter that the papers we had sent to the reporter were fake and would not be found in her school records.

So the reporter went to the school himself to check Jennifer's claim that the documents weren't fake. On the local news broadcast the reporter said that the school did have the same papers as the ones we had sent the reporter.

The reporter went on to say that he had checked the school records himself and confirmed that Jennifer had reported a bogus radical mastectomy to the school. This story was sent down to the station's affiliate in Orlando and a reporter in our area called to ask if we had heard the latest news about Jennifer.

We told the reporter that we had and that it was us that sent the original information to their affiliate up in Jacksonville. The reporter said how bad he felt for this child and that Jennifer had been out of work at this point for nine months. How was she taking care of this baby – not to mention her own children – if she wasn't working?

The reporter told us this might be something that we should report to Child Protective Services. We sent the news clip to a prior attorney, the second one we had worked with, early on in the case. We asked if he would take our case again. He felt that first we should file a complaint against our former attorney who was already in jail awaiting a hearing for fraud.

This attorney thought filing a complaint with the Florida Bar Association against our former attorney would possibly help us to get a whole new trial. Because of his incompetence, our former attorney had lost us any chance we might have had to be able to appeal our case and get our daughter. On top of that, he was also putting information related to our case on the Internet, even though our case was still ongoing. This violated the client-attorney privilege.

The attorney felt that we had a good case against the midwife and OB/GYN for not following the Florida statute for doing a surrogacy. We also had a good case for the Florida Supreme Court, because Tom's civil rights had been violated according to the state constitution.

So now we are awaiting a court date in the county we live in to proceed with fraud charges against Jennifer, as well as the other cases against the midwife, the OB/GYN, and the civil rights violation. The judge did not have the right to take away Tom's right to be a parent, especially he never signed away his parental rights.

Because of our perseverance, our case is being discussed in the Florida legislature and they are looking for ways to remedy what has happened to us and other couples around this nation. It is our hope that this will indeed become a reality, and not just talk. And if we can help, we will.

# Chapter 10

# Final Thoughts

Did Jennifer and Sue find a loophole in the law by faking a surrogacy, knowing they could not sue a sperm donor for child support in the state of Florida – but could sue the intended father in a traditional surrogacy? Where we thought Jennifer and her attorneys made a mistake was Jennifer stating she didn't want us in the child's life and didn't put Tom as father on the birth certificate.

Since the surrogacy contract did not follow the Florida statutes, this could have and would have been the judge's only conclusion – that my husband was treated by Jennifer more like a sperm donor than an intended father in a surrogacy contract. If you remember, Jennifer did not put Tom on the birth certificate or give the child our last name.

So we end up paying no child support and get no visitation or parental rights. This was not what Jennifer and her attorneys were going for, and it definitely was not going to get them what they wanted. Jennifer's attorneys were hoping – like other attorneys in Florida told us – that whoever did not get permanent or primary custody would have to pay child support.

Under the Florida Statutes Chapter 63 at 63.062 [1], because the judge terminated or denied the father the right to be the father of the child, the judge violated the right to parent a child without intrusion under the constitution of the state of Florida. An outside attorney watching our case in the news alerted us to this violation of Tom's rights. Attorneys across Florida and the country were left scratching their heads. How could my husband be a sperm donor?

This case should have been equivalent to a one night stand since the surrogacy contract did not follow the Florida statutes according to outside attorneys watching this case as it unfolded. This case should have become simply a matter of who gets custody and who pays child support. Yes, it was true that looking back on this case, we took it for granted that the laws for surrogacy in the state of Florida would protect us.

Because we had done a surrogacy before and used the same contract and everything went as it was supposed to, we dropped our guard. Big mistake! If there is one thing that I can convey to intended parents and surrogates it is be careful – take the time not only to get to know each other, but to get a lawyer. Don't do it yourself. Take precautions to remedy in writing any problems that could possibly happen.

Tom and I believe, even after all that we have been through, that surrogacy can be a very good alternative for parents who are not able to conceive on their own. With surrogacy as well as adoption you run the risk that the mother can always change her mind at the last minute and keep the baby. It is up to the individual parents whether they feel this is a risk worth taking.

We thought that it was. We felt that even if the surrogate decided to keep the baby at the end, we could work this out with some kind of co-parent arrangement. If this is something that you would agree with as intended parents, be sure that you convey this to your attorney and the surrogate and put it in writing. We have been told, "Boy, you sure were suckers," and how we made a big mistake doing it the way we did.

But we feel that if you learn a lesson and you never repeat the mistake, then the mistake was not in vain. We are not giving up hope that if things don't work out and our child looks back and wonders if her father ever wanted her, she will find through this book and various other media that her father fought diligently to get her; he was a father who had planned to love her and take care of her forever. If this book saves others from the heartache that we have been through it will have been worth writing. For Tom this book was therapy, but for me it was a way of warning others to beware of the scams and fraud that are going on with surrogacies.

It seems that no matter what you do, or how well you try to protect yourself, somebody comes up with a way to get around it. My hopes are that before our story ends we help improve the surrogacy laws. Most of all, we would like to thank everyone for all their thoughts and prayers, because without our faith in God I know we would not have been able to endure these long two years, and counting, fighting this fight.

When we were weary and felt like we could not go on, we prayed and found through our faith that when we were not strong enough, God was. So now we are carrying on and are planning to do another surrogacy. We plan to use the frozen eggs we had left over from our first surrogacy journey. This time we'll be much smarter and take nothing for granted. God bless you all.

Resources

# Documents

Breach of contract letter sent to surrogate.

Breach of Traditional Surrogacy Contract

To: ██████████████████████

This is an acknowledgement of a material breach of contract after confirmation of pregnancy as stated in Paragraph B of the Traditional Surrogacy Contract, on the part of the surrogate ████████████████████ ( hereinafter referred to as the "Surrogate") and the intended father ██████████████ ( hereinafter referred to as the "Intended Father") and the intended mother ████████████████ ( hereinafter referred to as the "Intended Mother") The Intended Father and the Intended Mother are hereinafter collectively referred to as Intended Parents.

As in the Traditional Surrogacy Contract paragraph H and sub-paragraph number 3 states that the surrogate agrees not to smoke any type of cigarettes, drink alcoholic beverages, or use illegal drugs, prescription or non prescription drugs without the consent of the obstetrician or midwife. It has been confirmed by midwife that she did not give surrogate consent to smoke any cigarettes for Migraines or any other condition as it could be un-healthy for the un-borned child. Surrogate has confirmed that she does smoke cigarettes and has been since time of pregnancy.

This letter of breach of contract between surrogate and intended parents is in compliance with the Traditional Surrogacy Contract and is to inform the surrogate of such a breach in writing. The surrogate has stated that the breach can not be cured that she will continue smoking for her alleged migraines.

It is the intentions of the Intended Parents to take legal responsibility of the child and adoption at time of birth as long as said child is the biological child of the intended father and the child is checked out by a Physician at time of birth and found to be healthy with no abnormalities do to smoking cigarettes. At that time if the child is healthy and you sign the rescind ion form to give up any legal ties to this child the Intended Parents agree to pay the surrogate her surrogacy fee of $15,000 minus the $1500.00 first payment that was already paid to the surrogate. The Intended Parents will also pay for maternity clothes at 12 weeks as agreed. Also as it states in the original contract we will send

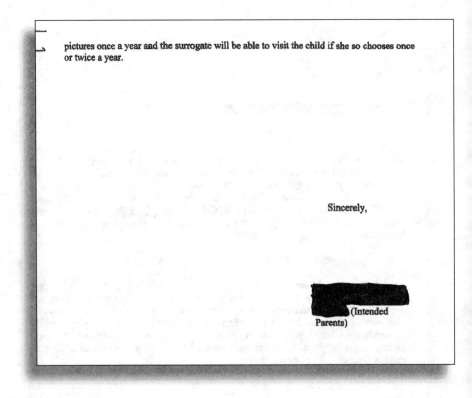

pictures once a year and the surrogate will be able to visit the child if she so chooses once or twice a year.

Sincerely,

(Intended Parents)

# Breach of contract response from surrogate.

>
>Here is my response to your breech of contract

>1) It states that my midwife did not give me consent to smoke any >cigarettes for migranes or any other condition.... This statement is >untrue. She did infact give me permission to smoke cigarettes as >alternative treatments to cure the migranes are considered more dangerous >that that of smoking cigarettes.
> Further, ███ would not need to give me permission or consent as the >FDA states that smoking less than 10 cigarettes per day should be >considered "safe" at any stage of pregnancy, as per ███.

>2) I have decided to change doctors as no doctor needs to play "in >between". I have further decided to not inform you of the new doctor of my >choosing until after requested DNA testing confirms that you are the >biological father of the child. Being that you are requesting the >paternity testing, you have relinquished yourself from the priviledge of >contacting my doctor during the pregnancy until after confirmation. At >such time, someone will contact you to inform you of whom my new doctor is.
> Due to the change in doctors, I will no longer qualify for a home birth >since ███ is the only certified midwife in Jacksonville and some >surrounding counties. In the original contract, it states that if I give >birth at home, I will recieve a compensation fee of $15,000; if I deliver >at a birthing center, I will recieve a $18,000 compensation fee; if I >deliver in a hospital, I will recieve a $20,000 compensation fee. >Therefore, due to the change in doctors, we are no longer looking at the >$15,000 compensation fee.
>
>3) It states in the Breech of contract that it is your intention to take >legal responsibility at the time of birth if the child is checked out by a >physician at the time of birth and found to be healthy with no >abnormalities due to smoking cigarettes. You can have a doctor of your >choosing to perform a physical on the baby, I also have the right to choose >a doctor to perform the same or a similar test. Any findings must be >backed by research documentation to prove that cigarettes alone caused any >abnormalities.
>
>4) It states in the Breech that the surrogate has stated that the breech >cannot be cured that she will continue smoking for her alleged migranes. >This is not completely true, and as stated is untrue. I have stated to you >on the phone that I am willing to stop smoking cigarettes if you will sign >a statement agreeing to allowing me to take necessary prescription >medications to cure the migranes. Taking nothing is not an option as my >general physician has stated that it is a hazard to my health.
>
>5) Please do not contact me other than email. Please do not contact my >workplace, my friends or any relatives past or present. Defamation of >character and slander is a crime.
>
>6) It states that you will pay the surrogate the surrogate fee (which now >needs to be adjusted due to the change in doctors). I am >sending you this letter and a check for $1500 (to repay this first payment) >as well as the other $500 you requested to repay you for gas money, food, >etc. Please do not send me any further finances including maternity >clothing allowance at 12 weeks gestation. Any further finances can be paid >at time of birth or completion of DNA testing upon confirmation of >paternity. In other words, I do not want any money from you until after >confirmation of paternity whatsoever. Contact must be limited to email or >USPS mail effective immediately.
>
>I am sending this letter and the check, as stated above, via certified >mail.
>
>███
>Sent via email 10-24-06 at 7:40 p.m. EST
>
>
>███
> These are the papers I am sending you thru the mail of our >intentions...Thanks Tom
>

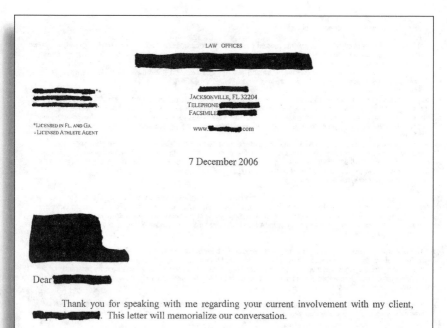

LAW OFFICES

████████████████████

████████████

*LICENSED IN FL. AND GA.
- LICENSED ATHLETE AGENT

JACKSONVILLE, FL 32204
TELEPHONE ████
FACSIMILE ████

www.████com

7 December 2006

Dear ████████

Thank you for speaking with me regarding your current involvement with my client, ████████. This letter will memorialize our conversation.

As we discussed, my client has suggested you have challenged the paternity of the child she currently carries. You have suggested that if this is your child you would like to take custody of it upon birth. You also suggested that if this is not your child you are not interested in being involved with the child. To clarify this issue a paternity test is required. As the child is not born this test will involve a surgical procedure. My client has verified that she has scheduled this test and made you aware of the timing and costs involved. You responded that you are not available. It is my understanding of this procedure that your involvement is minimal and that collection of your genetic sample can be accomplished through contracted medical service professionals wherever you may be at the time. As such I hereby request you contact this office regarding your availability and whereabouts to accomplish this goal.

Another issue is the cost involved. As a participant we hereby request you contribute ½ of the cost involved and, if your paternity is established, ask that you reimburse the other ½ of the costs at that time. These costs have been confirmed from the lab - ████████████████████ ████████████████████ and a formal invoice can be provided directly from the lab following the procedure. It is unclear whether this quoted cost is simply for the procedure to be performed on my client only, or inclusive of your test as well. Regardless, we request ½ of the total amount.

We also discussed your willingness to proceed if you are the genetic parent. You referenced a contract which you believe controls the issue. I have not been able to verify that a contract exists in this matter. Please be aware that my client contends that there is no contract. As such, if your paternity is established, we will need to proceed with drafting a contract to control the future relationship between yourself and my client. I highly recommend you seek the advise of counsel in this matter and forward my information to your lawyer for future negotiations.

In the meantime, please contact my office regarding your availability of the genetic test. This is necessary to understand which issues must be addressed. As you can see time is of the essence as my client continues to develop this child and it will arrive regardless of our scheduling. Please contact me to make arrangements as soon as possible to avoid unnecessary litigation and legal procedures.

Should you have any questions regarding the foregoing, please do not hesitate to contact me.

Very truly yours,

For the Firm

MSB/
cc:

# Letter from Surrogate's Attorney, dated January 18, 2007

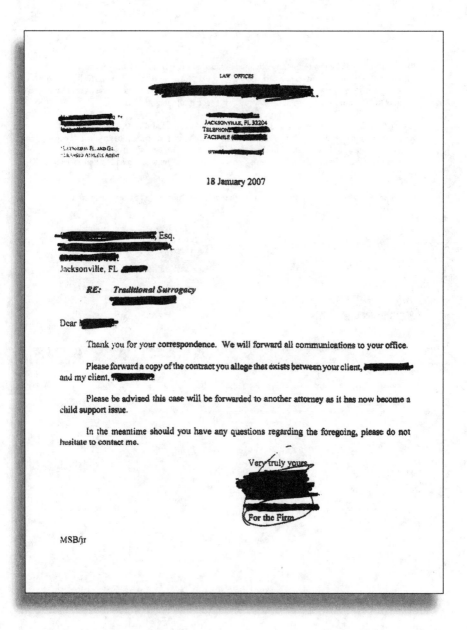

LAW OFFICES

JACKSONVILLE, FL 32204
TELEPHONE
FACSIMILE

LICENSED FL AND GA
LICENSED ATHLETE AGENT

18 January 2007

████████, Esq.

Jacksonville, FL ████

**RE:     Traditional Surrogacy**

Dear ████:

Thank you for your correspondence. We will forward all communications to your office.

Please forward a copy of the contract you allege that exists between your client, ████████ and my client, ████████.

Please be advised this case will be forwarded to another attorney as it has now become a child support issue.

In the meantime should you have any questions regarding the foregoing, please do not hesitate to contact me.

Very truly yours,

For the Firm

MSB/jr

Letter from Surrogate's Attorney, turning the case over to a new firm.

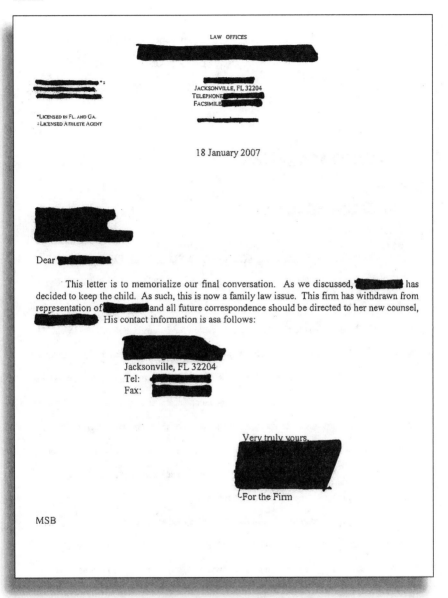

LAW OFFICES

████████████████████████████

████████████████ *‡
████████████████

*LICENSED IN FL. AND GA.
‡ LICENSED ATHLETE AGENT

JACKSONVILLE, FL 32204
TELEPHONE ██████████
FACSIMILE ██████████

████████████

18 January 2007

████████████████████
████████████████████

Dear ████████████

  This letter is to memorialize our final conversation. As we discussed, ██████████ has decided to keep the child. As such, this is now a family law issue. This firm has withdrawn from representation of ██████████ and all future correspondence should be directed to her new counsel, ██████████ His contact information is asa follows:

████████████████████

Jacksonville, FL 32204
Tel: ██████████
Fax: ██████████

Very truly yours,

████████████████

For the Firm

MSB

IN THE CIRCUIT COURT, FOURTH
JUDICIAL CIRCUIT, IN AND FOR
DUVAL COUNTY, FLORIDA

CASE NO.: ███████████

DIVISION:   FM-E

IN RE: THE MATTER OF

███████████ Petitioner,

and

███████████ Respondent.

## ORDER DENYING
## SECOND EMERGENCY MOTION FOR CUSTODY AND VISITATION

This cause came before the Court on July 31, 2007 on the Respondent's Second Emergency

Motion for Custody and Visitation. The Court took testimony from the parties and received

evidence. This case comes to the Court on the Petition for Determination of Paternity filed by

███████████ the birth mother. The Respondent, ███████████ has filed an Answer and

Counter Petition. The Petitioner moved to dismiss the Counter Petition and that motion was also

set for hearing on July 31, 2007, however, at the commencement of the hearing the Petitioner

announced that she had agreed to withdraw the motion since the Respondent had agreed to file an

Amended Answer and Counter Petition. Therefore, the Court proceeded with the hearing on the

Second Emergency Motion for Custody and Visitation. Based upon the testimony and evidence

presented, the Court makes the following findings:

     A.    The testimony reveals that the Petitioner placed an online ad volunteering to act as

a surrogate mother for the birth of a child. The Respondent responded to the online ad and the

parties engaged in discussions concerning him providing sperm to impregnate her with a child. He testified that the Petitioner provided him with a written agreement which he signed and had his soon to be wife sign and returned it to the Petitioner for her signature. He stated that she told him that she had received it and signed it and also that she would send him a copy but she never did. She testified she never signed the agreement. During the hearing, neither party had a copy of the agreement which was signed by the intended father and mother nor the surrogate. Counsel for the Respondent stated that he had a copy of the agreement signed by the Respondent and his soon to be wife and he asked to supplement the record by submitting that after the hearing. He has done so and the document which appears to be an identical copy of the unsigned document that was proffered during the hearing, with the addition to having the signatures of the Respondent and his soon to be wife, is marked as Respondent's Exhibit 4.

B.      The intended parents signed the contract September 6, 2006. Apparently, at that time, the surrogate was already impregnated. The child was born on May 9, 2007. During the pregnancy, the parties began to have disagreements. The intended father questioned whether he was actually the biological father of the child and requested a DNA test to confirm this. He also alleged that the surrogate was in material breach of the contract by smoking cigarettes and having unprotected sexual intercourse. She became concerned as to the father's moral and emotional stability. In October, 2006 the intended father communicated to the surrogate that he believed that she was in material breach of the contract. On November 23, 2006, he emailed her and stated "████ (intended mother) wants me to do the test and she wants the baby. On the other hand I don't. I want to end this here and now. So I will need time to work this out. It may take a week or months I don't know. I will let you know once I do." In January, 2007 she says she revoked and terminated the agreement.

C.      In reviewing the Pre-Adoption Plan Contract, Respondent's Exhibit 4, the Court notes

2

that there are several provisions that do not comply with § 63.213, Fla. Stat. or are in contravention of that statute. Specifically, subsection (e) of the statute requires that the intended father and intended mother acknowledge that they may not receive custody or parental rights under the agreement if the volunteer mother terminates the agreement or if the volunteer mother rescinds her consent to place her child for adoption within 48 hours after birth. Subsection (i) states, "That the agreement may be terminated at any time by any of the parties." The contract provides in paragraph III(A)(6) "The Surrogate or the Intended Parents may withdraw their consent to this Agreement and may terminate this Agreement with written notice given to the other party anytime prior to conception by the Surrogate subject to the provisions provided below." In subparagraph (g) of the statute, it is provided "that the intended father and intended mother agree to accept custody of and to assert full parental rights and responsibilities for the child immediately upon the child's birth, regardless of any impairments of the child." The Pre-Adoption Plan Contract, Respondent's Exhibit 4, provides for that language in paragraph III(F), however, paragraph III(O)(B) Material Breach of Contract After Confirmation of Pregnancy, states that if the Surrogate is the breaching party and if after the birth of the child, the child is not healthy and/or is abnormal as a result of the Surrogate's breach, then all compensation and reimbursement shall be forfeited by the Surrogate. This contradicts subparagraph (g) of the statute and paragraph III(F) of the contract. This provision also appears to be in contravention of § 63.213(3)(a), Fla. Stat. which provides that a Pre-Plan Adoption Agreement shall not contain any provision to "reduce any amount paid to the volunteer mother if the child.... is born alive but impaired".

D.    As a result of the foregoing observations, the Court has serious concern as to whether or not there was an executed contract, a meeting of the minds or a contract that complies with that

3

Statute. Additionally, § 742.14, Fla. Stat., provides that the donor of any ......sperm...., other than.....a father who has executed a Pre-Planned Adoption Agreement under § 63.212, Fla. Stat., shall relinquish all maternal or paternal rights and obligations with respect to the donation of the resulting children. In the case of Lamaritata v. Lucas, 823 So. 2d 316 (Fla. 2nd DCA, 2002), the Court made it clear that a donor who was not a commissioning couple or a father who has executed a Pre-Planned Adoption Agreement had no parental rights. As such the Court believes that it is inappropriate to establish custody or provide for visitation between the child and the Respondent until these issues have been determined by the Court.

It is, therefore

**ORDERED AND ADJUDGED:**

1.      The Respondent's Second Emergency Motion for Custody and Visitation be and the same is hereby DENIED until such time as the Court makes a ruling on the threshold issue of whether or not the Respondent's Exhibit 4 is a duly executed and binding Pre-Planned Adoption Agreement as required by and in compliance with § 63.213, Fla. Stat. which was not revoked by the parties at any time prior to birth of the child. The Court believes that the parties should be allowed to present whatever additional evidence, if any, they may have with regard to these threshold issues and will schedule a hearing thereon upon request of either party.

**DONE AND ORDERED** in Chambers at Jacksonville, Duval County, Florida, this 3 day of August, 2007.

Circuit Judge

4

# Letter from the Lamitina's Attorney, dated September 13, 2007.

**Sent:** Thursday, September 13, 2007 2:59 PM
**To:**
**Subject:** ▬▬▬▬▬▬

▬▬:

After we left the hearing yesterday I had thoughts and concerns over the letter that ▬▬ allegedly sent on Jan.18. I would like to discuss it with you. I have concerns over why it was not attempted to be entered into evidence through ▬▬. You tried to get it in through every other witness, but not through the author who was in the courtroom.

It is making me question the authenticity of the letter and why ▬▬ didn't testify that he wrote it. If this is lawyer's strategy, that is one thing, but I am having concerns of whether that letter was actually mailed.

Please let me know and settle my assurances that the letter was not a fraud and was attempted to be entered into evidence through everyone but the author, and why you made reference to it in your closing when it was never admitted into evidence.

This is a matter of great concern and very important as I need to know these answers to satisfy my ethic al responsibilities to the Court and to the Florida Bar. I am sure that you can appreciate my position and why I need these concerns set aside.

Thank you.

▬▬▬▬

# Surrogate's irrevocable letter of resignation.

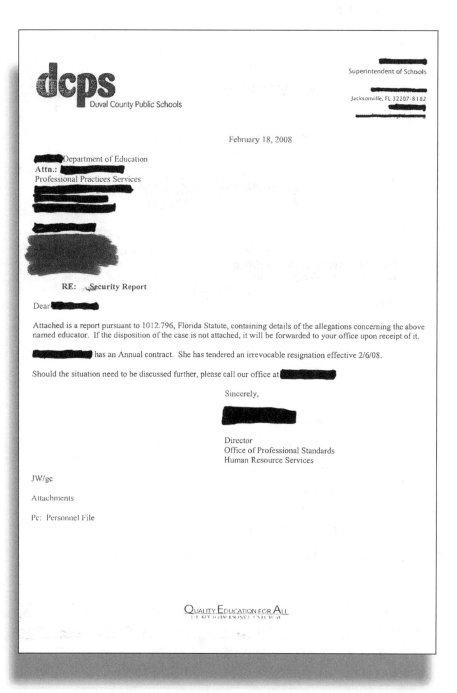

**dcps**

Duval County Public Schools

Superintendent of Schools

Jacksonville, FL 32207-8182

February 18, 2008

██████Department of Education
**Attn.:** ████████
Professional Practices Services

████████████

████████████
██████████████

**RE:** Security Report

Dear ██████

Attached is a report pursuant to 1012.796, Florida Statute, containing details of the allegations concerning the above named educator. If the disposition of the case is not attached, it will be forwarded to your office upon receipt of it.

██████████ has an Annual contract. She has tendered an irrevocable resignation effective 2/6/08.

Should the situation need to be discussed further, please call our office at ██████████

Sincerely,

████████████

Director
Office of Professional Standards
Human Resource Services

JW/gc

Attachments

Pc: Personnel File

QUALITY EDUCATION FOR ALL

Professional Standards Office notice of bogus radical mastectomy claim by surrogate.

---

**MEMORANDUM**

TO: ██████████████████
Professional Standards
Human Resource Services

FROM: ████████████ Technical Manager
Professional Standards Office

SUBJECT: **PERSONNEL INVESTIGATION INVOLVING**
████████████████ **TEACHER**
**SOCIAL SECURITY**████████████

DATE: 02-05-08

The Office of Professional Standards began an investigation on 01-15-08 involving ████████████ S.████████████ who reported a bogus radical mastectomy to her Principal Ms.████████████████ a return to work Doctor's note requesting light duty. The Doctor's note was a forgery on letterhead which was generated from Dr.███ ████████ web-site. The Doctor's note was not even a good facsimile.

████████████████ submitted an **Irrevocable Letter of Resignation effective 02-06-08.**

As a result of the investigation, the allegation is cleared as:

☐ **UNFOUNDED**: Evidence shows allegation(s) has/have no merit.

☒ **SUSTAINED**: Evidence proves allegation(s) to be true.

☐ **UNABLE TO PROVE OR DISPROVE:** Cannot sustain that the allegation can proved or disproved.

☐ **CLEARED BY ARREST**: The employee was arrested.

If you need further assistance, please contact me at 390-2054.